FOOD FOR THOUGHT

SECOND EDITION

FOOD FOR THOUGHT
SECOND EDITION

by   T. P. LABUZA, Ph.D.

Professor, Food Technology,
Department of Food Science
and Nutrition,
University of Minnesota

and   A. ELIZABETH SLOAN, Ph.D.
Communications Specialist,
Nutrition Department,
General Mills, Inc.,
Minneapolis, Minnesota

THE AVI PUBLISHING COMPANY, INC.

WESTPORT, CONNECTICUT

© *Copyright 1977 by*
THE AVI PUBLISHING COMPANY, INC.
Westport, Connecticut

Library of Congress Cataloging in Publication Data

LaBuza, T   P
  Food for thought.

  (Avi textbook series)
  Bibliography: p.
  Includes index.
  1. Food. 2. Nutrition. I. Sloan, Anne Elizabeth,
joint author. II. Title.
TX353.L2 1977   641.1   77.7131
ISBN 0-87055-244-9

Printed in the United States of America

Dedication

To my mother, Catherine, who persevered through every imaginable problem I caused her. She cannot fully be repaid for the time and devotion she has given me. I hope this book will fill the gap.

Preface To The Second Edition

I have been pleased with the acceptance of this book and the response of students to it.

This Second Edition has been updated to accommodate changes since 1974 and selected illustrative matter has been added to the text where appropriate.

March 1, 1977   Theodore P. Labuza

Preface To The First Edition

The science of nutrition and knowledge about food is based on the ancient Greek philosophy which states that one should *know thyself*. This can be restated in a modern maxim which many competent nutritionists, as well as many food faddists, have quoted. This statement, "You are what you eat," presents the same sound philosophy as that of the ancient Greeks, and is the basis for this book.

Technically, if a person is to be educated about what he needs for proper nutrition he must have a combined knowledge of biochemistry, physiology, food chemistry, and food processing. However, the purpose of this book is not to present a textbook of chemical equations and formulas, but to provide sound information about food and nutrition in an interesting and easy-to-read format. Too many people define nutrition as *eating what you don't like because you know it's good for you*. It is the purpose of this book to dispel this type of reasoning and to replace it with a knowledgeable approach to what we eat and why.

This book will attempt to provide an overview of nutritional concepts and food science theories so that individuals can learn to make sound judgments about the quality of a particular diet or the usefulness of a particular food. This can only be accomplished if something is learned about the interactions of the food components during digestion and the chemical needs of the body. Those areas of the greatest interest and those which can be easily understood without a background in biochemistry and science will be covered. The first part of this book is designed to teach nutrition on the basis of body requirements. The fascinating interrelationships of nutrients, which are vital in terms of physical well-being, are discussed. The rest of the book will cover the how and why of food processing, especially the effects of processing on nutritional value and the safety of food additives. With this information it is hoped that the reader can better evaluate his own concepts about food.

Many people have no understanding of food values, what nutrition is, why foods are processed, or what food processing entails. This lack of education has become even more evident in recent times. Articles written by those who have little knowledge of food science are continually condemning the food industry and the Food and Drug Administration. Literally hundreds of new fad diets sponsored by people who have not been trained in nutrition are appearing on the market. Youth has turned away from the *plastic-instantized-commercial* foods and is searching for the *natural-organic-traditional* foods. They do this without any real knowledge of the food industry and with a lack of understanding about what is meant by *good nutrition*. Overall, from the hippie to the housewife, the national outlook appears to be totally confused about what food and proper nutrition is all about.

Unfortunately, this lack of knowledge has a sound basis. Most of our population was only briefly reminded about the importance of the *basic four* or the *basic seven* during their grade school or high school career. In all probability many were never taught about the concepts behind these food guide-lines and, consequently, are unable to apply them effectively. In addition, many of the teachers responsible for this subject matter have had this teaching responsibility thrust upon them when there was no one else available. They are not trained in this area and, therefore, are not competent to teach about foods. Most education curricula on the college level do not require courses in nutritional concepts.

The realization of the lack of nutrition education that exists in the United States today is difficult to understand when we consider the importance of diet in our daily lives. While we must eat every day to stay alive, we can survive without a knowledge of mathematics, history, or the study of the ar-chitecture of ancient civilizations. However, our educational process has evolved in such a way that such subjects are given priority over the study of nutritional science. Perhaps this is because we believe nutrition is a subject covered in home economics courses, rather than the important basis for life that it is. How many male students ever learn anything about nutrition in high school, or for that matter, in college? The responsibility for the assimilation of this type of knowledge has traditionally been left to the female, and the job of teaching

her has not been adequate. Thus, the basis for the lack of
knowledge about nutrition is the poor education about nutrition
we have received. This must be changed. This book has been
written for that purpose. It is not a nutrition book for scientists
who are going to make a career of the study of nutrition; there
are many adequate books in that area. This book is for all
who want to know a little more about foods from a factual,
not a *fad* standpoint.

January 1974   T. P. LABUZA

Acknowledgements

This book has served a useful purpose to provide some sound information to many people unknowledgeable about food. Many have given me good suggestions for other books and revisions but most of all my wife Dr. A. Elizabeth Sloan has endeavored with me to bring the book up to date. I thank her immensely.

Contents

CHAPTER 1

Nutritional Adequacy

Characteristics of Nutritional Adequacy

What are some characteristics commonly attributed to nutritional adequacy (or inadequacy)? What state of mind or body makes us feel healthy and gives us vitality?

Size.—Though size with respect to normal body growth and development is most certainly affected by nutrition, many Americans have the general opinion that the concept *the bigger, the better* is true. For example, when a baby is born the first question, "Is it a boy or a girl?" is followed immediately by the second question, "How big is it?" Furthermore, as the reply to the second question increases in pounds, the opinion that the baby is a healthy one increases accordingly. This attitude is challenged by the introduction of data that indicate that a correlation may exist between *roly-poly* infants and fat adults.

The size parameter is also used when referring to Japanese who have grown up in the United States versus Japanese who were raised in Japan. The size comparison between these two groups reveals that the American-raised Japanese are larger in stature than the Japanese-raised. This is an accurate observation, but is this larger size desirable? Proponents of the importance of success in the Olympic games base much of the reason for the success of Americans upon their bigness and healthiness. Yet, in these same Olympic games, the smaller Japanese people are superior to their larger American counterparts, particularly in gymnastics and volleyball. The population of the village of Abkhazian in Georgia, a province of Russia, could be used as evidence to support another argument dispelling claims of the superiority of the bigger peoples. The people of Abkhazian are very short and fairly thin. Are they unhealthy? Considering that this village is one of the three areas of the world where a large percentage of the population lives longer than 100 years, it would be difficult to classify them as physically inferior. A quote from one of the inhabitants

1

of this village, Gabriel Chapnian, reveals his formula for lon-
gevity; "Long life equals active physical work plus a moderate
interest in alcohol and a moderate interest in the ladies."
(*National Geographic*, January 1973.)

However, size is still important considering that the thin,
frail child is more susceptible to disease and infection. The
question of size cannot be adequately answered since there are
more variables to be considered. We can state, however, as
will be seen, that obesity is not desirable, even though the
obese probably consume more than their share of an adequate
nutrient intake.

Stress.—A better criterion for determining nutritional adequacy is the effect of stress on a person. Stress effects may
result while the body is combating a disease or as the result of
emotional problems. A person who is nutritionally sound usually
does not fall apart under stress. He maintains sufficient stability to carry on bodily functions whether the stress results
from disease or an emotional condition. Observing the condition of the eyes, tongue, skin, liver, and thyroid when the body
is under stress can serve as a quick check for nutritional adequacy, but cannot give a total measure of nutritional adequacy.
This is an area in which we have problems defining adequacy,
because even the healthiest of us still become sick.

Intelligence.—A third criterion of nutritional adequacy is
intelligence. It has been determined that in the early life of a
child, IQ can be affected by the nutritional state to a high degree
and in later life to a lesser degree. Evidence of these effects
have been observed in areas of South and Central America,
Asia, and some regions of the United States where the poor
nutrition of the pregnant mothers resulted in pronounced negative effects on the learning ability of their children. Also,
children fed improperly at early ages had a lower intelligence-
testing ability. Further studies indicate that the negative effects
on learning and behavior caused by improper nutrition are
partially correctable. In these areas, diets are closely related
to the cultures of the people to a large degree; therefore, edu-
cating these people as to what constitutes a proper diet and the
subsequent implementation of better diets could eradicate many
of these nutritional deficiencies and hopefully improve the
mental abilities of the children.

Reproduction.—It is also evident that a strong correlation exists between the nutritional adequacy of a woman and her ability to reproduce. In those parts of the world where the mother has a nutritionally deficient diet, the number of birth defects, the number of stillborn births, the number of mis-carriages, and problems during child delivery are very high. This is a problem that can be alleviated by an adequate diet.

Biochemical and Clinical Analyses.—Lastly, we can also look at nutritional adequacy from the standpoint of real bio-chemical measurements. Blood, urine, and tissue samples can be analyzed and compared to established norms. Since nutrition is an infant science, the results of these tests are hard to in-terpret. In the past ten years, blood and urine analyses were performed on people in many parts of the United States in two major nutritional surveys. In some cases, hemoglobin levels in the blood and iodine levels in the urine were good indicators of nutritional status. However, for other nutrients, such as vita-min A or for blood protein level, no true direct correlation could be found with nutritional status. We can only estimate a pattern. In the future, when we understand nutritional science better, biochemical analyses of required nutrients will probably be an excellent method for assessing nutritional status.

When biochemical analyses are more interpretable, it will become possible to relate health problems to nutritional prob-lems. Certainly, moderate to severe deviations from the norm are evidence of nutritional problems, but problems such as lethargy or a headache cannot be tied directly to nutritional status.

Testing Problems.—There are several different parameters which can be utilized to determine nutritional adequacy: size, stress effects, intelligence, reproductive capabilities, and bio-chemical and clinical analyses. In addition, the testing of spe-cific diets can be utilized. However, a major problem exists when studying and testing specific diets, e.g., the effects of vitamins, minerals, etc. The problem is the ethical and moral question of making tests on humans. Should scientists or clini-cal nutritionists feed a pregnant mother a new diet to see if it affects the birth of her child? This is most certainly an unethical practice, but some studies using human subjects have been carried out. These practices should not be continued if they are dangerous. This leads to other problems: is it any more ethical to use animals for testing the nutritional adequacy of diets? And does the study of animals really give us useful information about man's diet?

Data collected from tests made on animals can be used and made applicable to humans when scaled to humans. The applicability of animal tests is easy under some conditions and extremely difficult under others. For example, the growth of an animal may be accurately correlated with the growth of a child or teenager. Diet studies related to reproduction may be effectively studied in animals and the results compared to the similar state in humans. But how is it possible to study the effects of diet on the intelligence of animals? Is it possible to accurately state that one animal is more intelligent than another if it can make a choice between two color plaques in a Skinner box, or can learn to run a maze? This kind of test may not be a proper criterion for studying intelligence, especially in relationship to diet.

Another problem is that many animals do not have the same biochemical pathway as humans. Simply put, this means that animals do not break down food into its various components and utilize them in the same manner as humans do. A good example of this dissimilarity between animals and man is found with the study of vitamin C.

Man is a very unusual animal in that the intake of vitamin C is required. Dogs, for example, do not require intake of vitamin C because they manufacture it themselves. Rats exhibit similar characteristics. Therefore, the effects of vitamin C on the nutritional adequacy of humans could not be studied by using dogs or rats: an animal that requires intake of vitamin C must be used. Fortunately, the guinea pig is an animal that does require intake of vitamin C, and it is used when studying the effects of vitamin C on humans. A problem occurs, however, in that we may still have some undiscovered essential nutrients that all animals make themselves, so that these nutrients are going to be difficult to discover and study.

Another question occurs: when we do feed a special diet to an animal, does the animal react in the same way a human would? It is a very difficult problem in animal studies to scale up the needs of animals to the needs of humans. Usually, when a special diet is studied, we prorate the intake of the test chemical in terms of milligrams (thousandths of a gram) of the food or nutrient per kilogram of body weight. If a rat is fed 1 mg/kg of body weight and the animal weighs 1 kg, then we would utilize this number when comparing it to a 70-kg man (140 to 150 lb). Therefore, we would feed 70 mg of the given nutrient. However, this type of correlation (animal to man) can be dangerous as exemplified by the following story.

There was a study done of the effects of LSD on man using animals as the research subjects. A researcher injected into an elephant a dose of LSD, in the amount that would effect a "high" in humans in terms of mg/kg of body weight. Since the elephant weighs many kilograms the dose of LSD was large. A half hour after the dose was administered, the elephant ran around in circles, trumpeted, defecated, rolled over, and died!

This type of research is unfortunate, but is an example of the effects of the scaling up or scaling down of dietary components or drugs in order to relate tests on animals to humans. Such types of direct correlation are not always valid, and therefore cannot be utilized with great accuracy. However, scientists and clinical nutritionists have no alternative except to use people, and as stated before, this practice could be considered unethical. Much research at the present time in nutrition is done using student volunteers. Because of this, the testing of extreme dietary concepts cannot be utilized due to the possibility of evoking extremely detrimental effects.

Prisoners are sometimes used for drastic diet experiments, but this is also a questionable practice. For example, Dr. R. M. Veatch of the Institute of Society, Ethics, and the Life Sciences reported on several experiments that have been done by others that he considers unethical. In one case, without their knowledge, normal female patients at a hospital were given drugs that caused abnormal heart beats. In another case, in a study of drugs for bronchial asthma among 130 children, 91 children received ineffective treatment for up to 14 years so that they would be the control group in the experiment. Fortunately, these types of tests are limited, since the question of ethics prevents studies like this from occurring. Recently, the use of the institutionalized, prisoners and the mentally ill, for nutritional studies has been questioned by the courts. However, it must be realized that if this type of research is discontinued progress in nutritional science will be slow.

The last major problem when studying the effects of diet on animals and man is tracing the biochemical breakdown of food

components. People usually say that it is difficult to find a
needle in a haystack. A scientific approach reduces the com-
plexity of this problem to a great extent. By burning the haystack and sifting the ashes, locating the proverbial needle is
very much simplified.

Another scientific search technique has been developed for
finding out how a chemical works in the body. The chemical is
labeled by making it very slightly radioactive. The chemical
is then fed to the animal or to man, the various tissues are
subsequently removed, digested by acid and heat, and then the
radioactive component is separated out and identified, much
like a radioactive needle in the body. This is a very useful tool
for detecting the location of the breakdown products of nutrients
and drugs in various tissues and organs of the body. Furthermore, it is possible that we can find out through these labeling
techniques what happens to these chemicals at the various locations in the body and thus learn their functions. This method
has led to many discoveries in new treatments of diseases.

Overall, it is evident that some means exist for utilizing
animals when studying nutritional adequacy in man, but in order
to understand more fully the status of a person in terms of
nutritional adequacy we must look at the human body.

The Body Is a Spiritual as Well as a Mechanical Machine

The human body may be separated into two different categories. Certainly, to many of us the major aspect of the human
body is its spiritual essence. This is the major consideration
from a religious standpoint; yet though it is a complete thought
process, it is very important from a nutritional standpoint
because spirituality or psychological state can be very much
affected by nutritional status. For example, emotional stress
can alter eating patterns and intestinal conditions. Digestion
can be affected to a great extent in a person who is undergoing
an emotional upset. Therefore, a sound spiritual state is important in terms of the diet and nutritional adequacy, although
scientists cannot measure this accurately; they must utilize
measurable conditions to determine the adequacy of a diet and
requirements of the body.

In order to attack nutritional adequacy from a scientific
approach, it is useful to consider that the body is an engine.

TABLE 1.1
CHEMICAL COMPOSITION OF THE BODY

	% by Weight
Carbon	18
Hydrogen	10
Oxygen	65
Nitrogen	3

An engine is a machine that requires an input (food) and creates an output (a waste product). As an engineer would look at it: input minus output causes some kind of change, an accumulation of something. In the human body the accumulation is energy. This energy is that power needed for maintenance, for move-ment, and for mental activity. The object is to maximize these accumulations to make the body very efficient. An interesting aspect of the human body is that it is a surprisingly efficient machine with the unique characteristic of being able to repair and make new parts, unlike many other machines. Of course, not all parts can be repaired. Brain cells cannot be replaced. But the body has the ability to repair injured tissues of most other organs.

In addition to possessing the qualities of an engine, the body is a conglomeration of chemicals. This is referred to as the *organic chemistry* or *biochemistry* of the body. The body is made up of a number of different chemicals which are very important in terms of their function and structure. The food we eat is the chemical input needed to repair, maintain, and to provide the energy necessary to carry on the body's life func-tions. Table 1.1 lists the major chemical components of the body as per cent by weight.

These chemicals make up almost 90% of the body, and since these chemical elements are the basis of organic chemistry, the human body is 90% organic. The rest of the body is com-posed of *inorganic* elements, or the minerals that make up the body. The importance of the inorganic chemicals will be re-viewed later in the book. For instance, calcium comprises al-most 2% of the body; when calcium is added to the carbon, hydro-gen, oxygen, and nitrogen in the body, these equal 98% of the to-tal body weight. Some other minor chemical elements which are

present in the body that are classified as minerals are phosphorus, potassium, sulfur, sodium, chlorine, and magnesium. The
total of these when added to the main five equals almost 99.9% of
total body weight. The rest of the body is composed of trace
amounts of other elements. Table 1.2 lists all the elements important to the body and the nature of their use in the body.
Trace amounts of 21 of the first 34 elements exist in the body.

As an example, from this table one of the elements, zinc, is needed
in minute amounts only. Since these low levels are difficult to
produce in experimental diets, no known need for zinc was
established until recently. A few years ago it was found that
there are places in the world where zinc is deficient in the diet
and this deficiency was evidenced by a nutritional syndrome.
This deficiency and others can be measured by a clinical nutritionist and, hopefully, can be corrected by the addition of
the deficient mineral or nutrient into the diet of the population
of the area.

It should be understood that the body is not a random combination of these various elements. In fact, they are combined
into compounds in a precise fashion in order to compose the
various organs of the body. Knowledge of the organs of the
body is necessary to understand how scientists measure the
nutritional adequacy of man. Blood, which is really an organ,
comprises about 8% of the total weight of the body; skin 7%;
liver 2.5%; and the brain 2.5%. The amount of muscle tissue
and fat tissue varies greatly.

The liver, muscle tissue and fat tissue are extremely important when studying the nutritional adequacy of a diet and
specifically, the nutritional status of a person. For instance,
if one consumes an excess of alcohol, it is found that the liver
grows in size and becomes fatty. Scientists studying the effect
of a diet on an animal may sacrifice (kill) an animal, dissect
it, remove and weigh the liver, and make a compositional
analysis of it. Muscle tissue, and the amount of fat tissue in a
human may also be examined. The amount of fat tissue in man
may vary from 17 to 72%. If a person has a body composed
of 70% fat, it is usually very evident from their appearance
that they have a form of nutritional disease. In the United
States 30% of the population is overweight; we live in a malnourished country, not because of a lack of proper nutrients,
but because of the over-intake of improper nutrients in an un-

TABLE 1.2
ELEMENTS RELATED TO NUTRITION

Element	Symbol	Atomic Number	Comments
Hydrogen	H	1	Required for water and organic compounds
Helium	He	2	Inert and unused
Lithium	Li	3	Probably unused
Beryllium	Be	4	Probably unused; toxic
Boron	B	5	Essential in some plants; function unknown
Carbon	C	6	Required for organic compounds
Nitrogen	N	7	Required for many organic compounds
Oxygen	O	8	Required for water and organic compounds
Fluorine	F	9	Growth factor in rats; possible constituent of teeth and bone
Neon	Ne	10	Inert and unused
Sodium	Na	11	Principal extracellular cation
Magnesium	Mg	12	Required for activity of many enzymes; in chlorophyll
Aluminum	Al	13	Essentially under study
Silicon	Si	14	Possible structural unit of diatoms; recently shown to be essential in chicks
Phosphorus	P	15	Essential for biochemical synthesis and energy transfer
Sulfur	S	16	Required for proteins and other biological compounds
Chlorine	Cl	17	Principal cellular and extracellular anion
Argon	A	18	Inert and unused
Potassium	K	19	Principal cellular cation
Calcium	Ca	20	Major component of bone; required for some enzymes
Scandium	Sc	21	Probably unused
Titanium	Ti	22	Probably unused
Vanadium	V	23	Essential in lower plants, certain marine animals and rats

TABLE 1.2 *Continued*

Element	Symbol	Atomic Number	Comments
Chromium	Cr	24	Essential in higher animals; related to action of insulin
Manganese	Mn	25	Required for activity of several enzymes
Iron	Fe	26	Most important transition metal ion; essential for hemo- globin and many enzymes
Cobalt	Co	27	Required for activity of several enzymes; in vitamin B_{12}
Nickel	Ni	28	Essentially under study
Copper	Cu	29	Essential in oxidative and other enzymes and hemocyanin
Zinc	Zn	30	Required for activity of many enzymes
Gallium	Ga	31	Probably unused
Germanium	Ge	32	Probably unused
Arsenic	As	33	Probably unused; toxic
Selenium	Se	34	Essential for liver function
Molybdenum	Mo	42	Required for activity of several enzymes
Tin	Sn	50	Essential in rats; function unknown
Iodine	I	53	Essential constituent of the thyroid hormones

balanced diet. Certainly, having 70% of the body weight com-posed of fat is also very dangerous for survival.

The other tissue that varies to a large extent from one person to another is muscle tissue. The range can be from 10 to 42% by weight. A football player may possess a large percentage of muscle tissue compared to body weight, but an average per-son does not have such a high percentage of muscle tissue. The proportions of muscle and fat tissue vary on the basis of the amount of food consumed.

The breakdown of these tissues reveals that the body is basi-cally composed of water. The body is almost 60% water, but the percentage of water varies among the different types of

TABLE 1.3
ORGAN COMPOSITION (%)

Organ or Tissue	H_2O	Solids	Protein	Lipid	Carbohydrate	Minerals
Muscle	72–78	22–28	18–20	3.0	0.6	1.0
Blood	79	21	19	1	0.1	0.9
Liver	68–80	20–40	15	3–20	1–15	1
Brain	78	22	8	12–15	0.1	1.0
Skin	66	34	25	7	trace	0.6
Bones	20–25	75–80	30	trace	trace	4.5

tissues under examination. For example, muscle tissue is about 75% water, about 20% protein, and about 3% fat. The composition of various organs is shown in Table 1.3.

Two kinds of nutrients are consumed, *essential* nutrients, such as vitamin C which must be consumed in the diet since the body cannot manufacture it, and *nonessential* nutrients. The intake of nonessential nutrients is not required, because the body can manufacture these from the essential nutrients by breaking them down into the various components required. As the body works harder in doing this, we must eat both essential and nonessential nutrients in a varied diet.

In order to demonstrate the need for a varied diet, the body can be compared to a cabbage. Man is 59 to 60% water, about 18% protein, 18% fat, traces of carbohydrates, and 4% minerals. These measurements have been determined by analyses of cadavers. The bodies are ground up into a fine comminuted product. If water content is to be measured, a portion of this product is put into a vacuum chamber, the water is extracted, and the weight of the remaining material is measured. Similarly, the protein and fat content can be determined. Measurements of the minerals that are left are obtained by putting a portion of this material into a hot oven (800°F) which burns off all the organic matter. The material left is a grey-white ash which is the amount of minerals that was present.

Cabbage is 92% water, 1.4% protein, 0.2% fat, and 6.3% carbohydrates. In Table 1.4 we can see a great difference in all areas

TABLE 1.4
GROSS COMPOSITION OF ORGANISMS (% PROXIMATE ANALYSIS)

Organism		H₂O	Protein	Carbohydrate	Lipid	Ash
Plants	Cabbage	92	1.4	6.3	0.2	0.8
	Onion	87	1.0	11.0	0.2	0.6
	Spinach	93	2.3	3.8	0.3	0.6
Microorganisms	*E. coli*	78	18.0	1.0	1.0	2.0
	Yeast	72	12.0	13.0	1.0	2.0
Invertebrates	Fly	73	20.0	3.0	3.0	1.0
	Scallop	80	15.0	3.4	0.1	1.4
Fish	Halibut	75	18.0	trace	5.2	1.3
Bird	Hen's egg	74	13.0	0.7	11.0	1.1
	Hen	56	21.0	trace	19.0	3.2
Mammals	Hog	58	15.0	trace	24.0	2.8
	Horse	60	17.0	trace	17.0	4.5
	Rat	60	30.0	trace	7.0	3.0
	Man	59	18.0	trace	18.0	4.0
Meat (cooked)	Hamburger	54	24.0	trace	20.0	2.0
	Steak	49	15.0	trace	36.0	0.7
Milk		87	3.5	4.9	3.7	0.7

compared to man. The cabbage has more water, 10 times less protein, much more carbohydrates, 90 times less fat, and 4 times less ash. In fact, the composition of man is closer to that of a horse or a pig. These would be ideal animals to use in nutritional studies except they are too large and cost too much to feed and maintain. The rat is the most common ex-perimental animal for nutrition studies. As seen in Table 1.4, the rat has much more protein than man and less than 50% of the fat. This could create a problem in scaling the research in rats to man, but so far it has not presented a serious handi-cap.

Animal Feeding Commonly Used In
Establishing Food Safety.

Overall, we have seen the problems involved in assessing nutritional status, since it is difficult and sometimes unethical to use man in an experiment. Animals are thus used even though they may respond differently and have a different body composition. From these studies with animals we have dis-covered and will discover what is needed by the body. These discoveries will be discussed in the following chapters.

CHAPTER 2

Nutrient Requirements and Energy

Discovery of Nutritional Requirements

The nutritional requirements of man were discovered through the study of anthropology, focusing on the causes of death in man. Anthropologists state that many of the deaths occurring in the Dark Ages were due to food poisoning or nutritional deficiencies. Many other deaths were due to the lack of medical care for such minor injuries as small cuts and bruises, which eventually became infected and resulted in death. It is probable that early explorers would have made their discoveries sooner had there been a greater awareness of nutritional requirements. For example, Vasco de Gama lost 60 out of 110 members of his ship's crew before he rounded the Cape of Good Hope as a result of nutritional disorders caused by diet deficiencies. Similarly, many anthropologists state that the discovery of the New World, India, and other places would have taken place earlier if people had really understood the nutritional require-ments of the body.

In Vasco de Gama's case, scurvy was the major disease that led to the high percentage of fatalities. Scurvy is a condition caused by the lack of vitamin C in the diet, causing stress on the body and the subsequent lowering of the body's resistance to disease. Death did not result directly from the lack of vita-min C, but from the contraction of pneumonia or some other malady.

Nutritional deficiencies were not confined to ancient times. The work of Pasteur revealed that milk carried brucellosis and tuberculosis bacteria, and that subjecting milk to a heat treatment killed these organisms. Within one year after pas-teurization was initiated, evidence of scurvy in children, es-pecially among those living in large cities, was apparent. The pasteurization process destroyed the vitamin C in the milk and even though milk contains very low levels of vitamin C, it was the main source for children at that time.

Beriberi, a paralysis disease caused by the lack of B vitamins, was also very common because of consumption of polished rice in many parts of the world. Rice was polished (hulls removed) as early as 2600 B.C. in order to make it last longer and taste better, but the polishing process also removed essential B vitamins. Japan, where a large rice-polishing industry thrived by the 1800's, lost almost 2000 out of 5000 sailors a year due to the prevalence of beri beri on board ship. The basic diet of these sailors consisted of white rice stripped of its B vitamins by polishing.

It has only been during the last 50 years that the basis of diseases caused by diet deficiencies has been discovered around the world. The major discoveries concerning vitamins occurred in the 1930's and the 1940's. It is only since that time that it has been possible to effectively treat deficiencies caused by improper diets. Thus the science of nutrition is relatively young and many new things are constantly being discovered.

Body Requirements

What are the specific requirements of the body in terms of nutritional status? The most important requirement of an adult is the ability to maintain body functions. In order to establish maintenance in the body three things are required: (1) a source of energy derived from foods high in fat or carbohydrates; (2) water; and (3) oxygen. These three elements alone could maintain a person for a long period of time, though deficiencies from a lack of the essential micronutrients would eventually develop.

Secondly, the body requires the ability to grow new tissues as well as maintain and repair itself. Growth capabilities are especially important for children, and the ability of the body to maintain and repair itself is a requirement for all ages. It is stated that approximately 1 billion cells per minute are under constant repair and replacement. In order to grow and repair cells, the intake of protein is essential. This process is sustained by the energy supplied by the intake of fats and carbohydrates. Vitamins and minerals are also essential. Fats, carbohydrates, water, oxygen, protein, vitamins, and minerals are essential for the building, repair, and maintenance of tissue such as bone and blood. The amounts of each

of these nutrients is important to the body, and they are measured in recommended requirements.

MDR and RDA.—MDR is an old term referring to the Minimum Daily Requirement. It is the amount of a specific nutrient
that supplies the needs to the average person. This was the
term originally used by nutritionists, but the misuse that resulted from the idea that if one unit of a given nutrient is the
minimum then two units is even better, made the term dangerous and useless. Therefore, this term has been eliminated
from use by the Food and Drug Administration and the new
term RDA referring to the Recommended Daily Allowance is
now utilized. These allowances set by the nutrition board of
the National Academy of Sciences—National Research Council
indicate the levels of vitamins, minerals, etc., that are recommended for 97.5% of the population in order to carry on maintenance, growth, and repair of the body. Table 2.1 lists the
RDA for the major nutrients required by the body. If one takes
in even two -thirds of the RDA, the body should be getting
enough because there is a large built-in safety factor. It is
only when the intake drops to a low value that a danger can
exist. It is also recognized that in most cases one can balance
out the intake over several meals or even days. In other words,
one -third of the RDA is not required at each meal.

Calories do Count: A Definition.—In Table 2.1 the first col-
umn of recommendations is caloric intake. Calories are a
measure of energy. A required amount of energy is necessary
for maintenance and growth of the body. From a scientific
standpoint, a small calorie is the amount of energy required to
raise 1 gm of water by $1^{O}C$ (about $1.8^{O}F$), *whereas a Btu is
the energy required to raise 1 lb of water by $1^{O}F$.* A large
Calorie, used when referring to food, is 1000 times as large
as a small calorie, or the amount of energy required to raise
1 kg (approximately 2.2 lb) of water by $1^{O}C$.

The exact amount of calories necessary for an individual
varies. For the adult it ranges from 2200 to 3000 Cal per day.
Obviously, the higher number is required by a person under
more stress or with a higher degree of physical activity. The
lower number would be required by a person whose physical
activity is less, for example, those with desk jobs. Over the
years daily life in the United States has been simplified by an
increase in mechanization, and caloric requirements have de

creased proportionately. For example, chopping wood was at one time part of the daily routine of many Americans, but as civilization progressed this type of physical exertion was no longer necessary. Men and women also exhibit varying caloric requirements. Women usually need fewer Calories than men due to their smaller body size and, in some cases, less strenuous work activities.

Calories are supplied by the components of food. Protein supplies some Calories (about 4 Cal/gm). The National Research Council recommends 46 to 56 gm of protein per day. This is the amount present in 10 oz of steak. Usually, 100 to 150 gm of protein per day are consumed by an average American; thus about 15% of the Calories in our diet come from protein. The recommended allowance for protein is currently under question by the National Research Council, since some nutritionists feel it is too high and can cause problems. Protein functions and requirements will be discussed in greater detail in a later chapter.

Carbohydrates, the sugars that supply energy, comprise about 35% of our caloric intake, but there is no recommended value. In order to meet energy needs, about 300 to 400 gm of carbohydrates should be consumed per day. Many researchers stress that this should not be in the form of simple sugars, but rather as more complex sugars in the form of starches.

Fats, another source of energy, comprise the remaining 50% of our caloric intake. Approximately 100 to 150 gm of fat are consumed in the average diet. Note the difference between fat and carbohydrates. Even though a lesser amount of fat is consumed, more energy per gram of fat is supplied to the body due to the difference between the way the body metabolizes fats and carbohydrates. Carbohydrates supply 4 Cal per gm, as does protein; fats supply 9 Cal per gm. For this reason diets utilized for purposes of weight reduction advocate the intake of lesser amounts of fats because of their larger caloric content. The high intake of fats is also under dispute by scientists because of the relation that has been shown between fat intake and heart disease. Many nutritionists feel that this should be reduced to 30 to 35% of the diet and that the type of fat consumed should be changed. This issue will be discussed in more depth in a later chapter.

Other Required Nutrients.—Micronutrients are additional

TABLE 2.1

FOOD AND NUTRITION BOARD, NATIONAL ACADEMY OF SCIENCES—

Designed for the maintenance of good nutrition

| | Age | Weight | | Height | | Energy | Protein | Fat-soluble Vitamins | | | |
| | | | | | | | | Vita-min A Activity | | Vita-min D | Vita-min E Activity[5] |
	(Yr)	(Kg)	(Lb)	(Cm)	(In.)	(Kcal)[2]	(Gm)	(RE)[3]	(IU)	(IU)	(IU)
Infants	0.0-0.5	6	14	60	24	kg × 117	kg × 2.2	420[4]	1,400	400	4
	0.5-1.0	9	20	71	28	kg × 108	kg × 2.0	400	2,000	400	5
Children	1-3	13	28	86	34	1,300	23	400	2,000	400	7
	4-6	20	44	110	44	1,800	30	500	2,500	400	9
	7-10	30	66	135	54	2,400	36	700	3,300	400	10
Males	11-14	44	97	158	63	2,800	44	1,000	5,000	400	12
	15-18	61	134	172	69	3,000	54	1,000	5,000	400	15
	19-22	67	147	172	69	3,000	54	1,000	5,000	400	15
	23-50	70	154	172	69	2,700	56	1,000	5,000		15
	51+	70	154	172	69	2,400	56	1,000	5,000		15
Females	11-14	44	97	155	62	2,400	44	800	4,000	400	12
	15-18	54	119	162	65	2,100	48	800	4,000	400	12
	19-22	58	128	162	65	2,100	46	800	4,000	400	12
	23-50	58	128	162	65	2,000	46	800	4,000		12
	51+	58	128	162	65	1,800	46	800	4,000		12
Pregnant						+300	+30	1,000	5,000	400	15
Lactating						+500	+20	1,200	6,000	400	15

Source: Natl. Acad. Sci.–Natl. Res. Council. (1974).

[1] The allowances are intended to provide for individual variations among most normal persons as they live in the United States under usual environmental stresses. Diets should be based on a variety of common foods in order to provide other nutrients for which human requirements have been less well defined. See text for more detailed discussion of allowances and of nutrients not tabulated.
[2] Kilojoules (kJ) = 4.2 × kcal.
[3] Retinol equivalents.
[4] Assumed to be all as retinol in milk during the first six months of life. All subsequent intakes are assumed to be half as retinol and half as β-carotene when calculated from international units. As retinol equivalents, ¾ are as retinol and ¼ as β-carotene.

requirements of the body, though in much smaller amounts; hence the term micro. For example, the amount of calcium required, though comprising almost 4% of the body, is about 1 gm per day or about 1/454 lb. Three glasses of milk will provide the necessary calcium required. Recent surveys show a lack of calcium in the diets of teenagers, adults, and senior citizens. Many people are under the mistaken impression that once bones are developed, calcium is no longer required. This is an incorrect assumption since calcium is constantly being metabolized by the body. A common malady of older people is osteoporosis, a softening of the bone due to lack of calcium in the diet and the subsequent dissolution of the bone.

NATIONAL RESEARCH COUNCIL RECOMMENDED DAILY
DIETARY ALLOWANCES,[1] Revised 1974
of practically all healthy people in the U.S.A.

Water-soluble Vitamins							Minerals					
Ascorbic Acid (Mg)	Folacin[6] (µg)	Niacin[7] (Mg)	Riboflavin (Mg)	Thiamin (Mg)	Vitamin B-6 (Mg)	Vitamin B-12 (µg)	Calcium (Mg)	Phosphorus (Mg)	Iodine (µg)	Iron (Mg)	Magnesium (Mg)	Zinc (Mg)
35	50	5	0.4	0.3	0.3	0.3	360	240	35	10	60	3
35	50	8	0.6	0.5	0.4	0.3	540	400	45	15	70	5
40	100	9	0.8	0.7	0.6	1.0	800	800	60	15	150	10
40	200	12	1.1	0.9	0.9	1.5	800	800	80	10	200	10
40	300	16	1.2	1.2	1.2	2.0	800	800	110	10	250	10
45	400	18	1.5	1.4	1.6	3.0	1,200	1,200	130	18	350	15
45	400	20	1.8	1.5	2.0	3.0	1,200	1,200	150	18	400	15
45	400	20	1.8	1.5	2.0	3.0	800	800	140	10	350	15
45	400	18	1.6	1.4	2.0	3.0	800	800	130	10	350	15
45	400	16	1.5	1.2	2.0	3.0	800	800	110	10	350	15
45	400	16	1.3	1.2	1.6	3.0	1,200	1,200	115	18	300	15
45	400	14	1.4	1.1	2.0	3.0	1,200	1,200	115	18	300	15
45	400	14	1.4	1.1	2.0	3.0	800	800	100	18	300	15
45	400	13	1.2	1.0	2.0	3.0	800	800	100	18	300	15
45	400	12	1.1	1.0	2.0	3.0	800	800	80	10	300	15
60	800	+2	+0.3	+0.3	2.5	4.0	1,200	1,200	125	18+[8]	450	20
80	600	+4	+0.5	+0.3	2.5	4.0	1,200	1,200	150	18	450	25

[5] Total vitamin E activity, estimated to be 80% as α-tocopherol and 20% other tocopherols.
[6] The folacin allowances refer to dietary sources as determined by *Lactobacillus casei* assay. Pure forms of folacin may be effective in doses less than 1/4 of the recommended dietary allowance.
[7] Although allowances are expressed as niacin, it is recognized that on the average 1 mg of niacin is derived from each 60 mg of dietary tryptophan.
[8] This increased requirement cannot be met by ordinary diets; therefore, the use of supplemental iron is recommended.

Another example is iron, which is required in the amount of
12 to 18 mg (a milligram is 1/1000 of a gram). Lack of iron
in the diet is a major source of a malnutrition disease in the
United States. Many girls and young women have low levels of
iron in their systems because of blood loss during menstruation. This leads to a form of anemia. A major controversy
at the present time is over the idea of increasing the percentage of iron added to bread. In the 1940's when this deficiency
was discovered in the United States, bread was used as the
mode of supplying the population with iron because at that time
bread consumption equaled 20% of the average diet. The consumption of bread is now much lower as a result of increased
intake of other foods; consequently, the issue of whether or not

increased levels of iron should be added to bread is under dispute, although the government has now required it.

Other micronutrients and their RDA are listed in Table 2.1
and will be discussed in Chapter 8. Overall, it is important to
remember that the amounts of all these requirements are
basically dependent upon age, sex, and levels of physical activity. The major problem that people have when choosing a correct diet is the fact that we are accustomed to eating food, not
requirements. It is my hope that this book may teach how to
balance a diet to meet our requirements.

Energy Requirements

Chemical energy is the energy obtained by the breakdown or
metabolism of foods. An energy supply to initiate this chemical
breakdown is vital as one of the food requirements. Mechanical
energy is that type of energy needed for the mechanical movement of the body. Thermal energy is a third energy requirement with the function of maintaining the body temperature. For
example, body temperature rises when the body is producing
chemical reactions to combat a disease. This results in a
fever. A normal body temperature must be maintained to enable
the body to carry on at maximum efficiency. Perspiring is
also an important function of the body that assists in regulating
body temperature by the evaporation of water. The opposite of
perspiring when the body is hot is shivering when the body is
cold. The process of shivering is the result of chemical reactions involving the burning of body sugars. This produces heat
which in turn is utilized to maintain body temperature. Therefore, perspiring and shivering are useful body functions and
are not merely reactions to heat and cold.

Electrical energy is required for such things as nerve transmission, the energy that is required for a nerve impulse to
travel down the nerve pathways. This electrical energy comes
from the chemical reactions of the nutrients we eat.

Efficiency of Body Functions.—Calculation of the efficiency of
the body's energy-producing characteristics yields a value of
only 30%, very much like that of the best machine available
today. This figure would seem to indicate that the body is not
a very efficient machine; however, it uses an additional 30%
of the energy available to maintain body temperature. A total

of 60% efficiency indicates that the body is in reality an extremely efficient machine.

Determination of Energy Values.— Food energy values are
measured by burning food in a device at high oxygen pressure;
the heat so generated is then measured. This device is called
a calorimeter.

Human energy requirements are made by putting a person
into a chamber equipped with thermocouples, devices for measuring temperatures. The inward flow of oxygen and the out-
ward flow of carbon dioxide are then measured, the heat loss
from the chamber is calculated, and by this process the body's
caloric requirements can be determined. The Basal Metabolic
Rate (BMR) is the minimum amount of energy in Calories per
hour required to maintain the body when it is undergoing no
voluntary actions. This amount of energy is the minimum
needed for the involuntary body functions, including blood flow,
breathing, peristalsis, and the electrical and chemical functions of the brain. It has been found that the BMR varies with
age, size, and sex. From birth to about 20 years of age the
caloric requirement is on the increase due to the body's growth
process, but from the age of 20 on up, basal energy requirements are on the decrease. Since eating habits are formed
during youth, obesity in older people is often based on the fact
that at 40 years of age a person may be using the same eating
habits that he learned at the age of 15, though he has a lower
BMR.

Men have higher requirements due both to size and activity.
The basal metabolic rate is 1200 to 1500 Cal per day for women
and about 1600 to 1800 per day for men. Diets that have a
caloric intake of less than 1200 Cal per day for women and
1600 Cal per day for men could cause stress on the body in
terms of failing to supply enough energy to maintain normal
body functions. Because of this, the body would have to burn
up fat and other tissues to supply the energy requirements.

Any activity over and above the BMR requires more Calories.
Table 2.2 lists some of the caloric values of various activities
in terms of total Calories spent.

A person sleeping 10 hours, eating 3 hours, and perhaps
watching television the rest of the time, would require only
about 1800 to 2200 Cal. Unfortunately, many people do live
such a sedentary existence, yet eat over 2500 Cal per day.

TABLE 2.2
CALORIC VALUES OF VARIOUS ACTIVITIES[1]

Activity	Cal/Hr	Cal/Min
Sleeping	60–100	1.0–1.2
Reclining		
(watching T.V.)	80–100	1.5–1.6
Eating	150	2.5
Driving a car	170	2.8
Shivering	300–400	5.0–6.7
Walking	300–350	3.8–5.8
Bicycling	350–500	4.5–8.3
Swimming	300–700	5.0–11.7
Handball	600–800	10.0–13.3
Running	700–800	11.7–13.3

[1] Includes BMR for average person.

Since 1 lb of body fat is equivalent to 3500 Cal, a person consuming an excess of 500 Cal per day could gain 1 lb every week. Exercise of any kind, even spaced over the whole day, would make up for this excessive intake. Two hours of vigorous walking or bicycle riding would be more than sufficient to burn the excessive intake of Calories. Of course, this is diffi-cult for many people to do, so they gain weight. The best an-swer is to reduce food intake and do a moderate amount of exercise as often as possible.

Overall, we have seen there are many different nutrient re-quirements, the most basic of which is energy. The Calories we eat do count, since they are needed to maintain body func-tions. If we take in too much food, it is converted to undesirable body weight. The important thing is to find the weight at which you function best and eat enough to supply that caloric need.

CHAPTER 3

Carbohydrates

Forms of Sugars

Carbohydrates (sugars and starches) supply 35 to 40% of the calories consumed in an average diet. Carbohydrates are present in many different foods and come in many different forms, most of which are interchangeable. These forms are illustrated in Fig. 3.1.

The first kind of sugars to be considered are the simple sugars. These sugars are made up of 6 atoms of carbon, 12 atoms of hydrogen, and 6 atoms of oxygen, as seen in the detailed structure. Two major types of simple sugars are glucose and fructose. They have exactly the same chemical content in terms of carbon, hydrogen, and oxygen, but are put together slightly differently (the OH groups are attached in different directions). All sugars digested by the body are eventually broken down into glucose. Fructose is readily converted to glucose in the body and glucose is the major sugar used by the cells for energy. Honey, as well as some syrups, has high concentrations of both glucose and fructose. Other kinds of foods may contain sugars that are more complex with regard to their chemical makeup.

Double sugars are made up of two simple sugars chemically combined. Sucrose is the most common example of a double sugar. Table sugar (sucrose) that is made from sugar cane and sugar beets is a double sugar composed of one molecule of glucose connected to one molecule of fructose, and has a very high level of sweetness. The body breaks down this double sugar into glucose and fructose during digestion; the fructose is in turn converted to glucose and the glucose is then utilized by the body for energy production as well as synthesis of other chemicals.

Another double sugar common in the diet is lactose. Lactose is the natural sugar found in both cow's and mother's milk. Lactose (milk sugar) is made up of a molecule of glucose and a molecule of galactose, which has a structure very similar

23

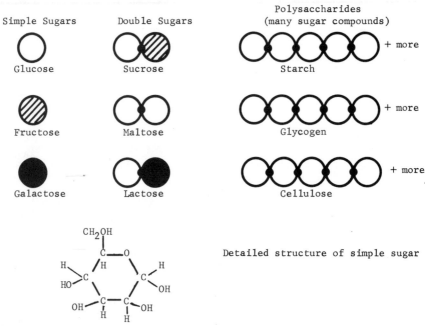

FIG. 3.1. CARBOHYDRATES (SUGAR STRUCTURE)

to glucose. Lactose is an unusual sugar in that only certain races of people in the world are able to digest it. North Americans and Western Europeans are fortunate in possessing the ability to digest lactose; however, in many parts of the world, including the Middle East, the Orient, and the African nations, people beyond their teens have difficulty digesting this sugar. This problem is created by the absence of a mechanism in the digestive tract for breaking down this sugar. As a result, the sugar passes from the stomach into the intestine where bacteria begin to ferment the sugar, and gas, diarrhea, and other problem conditions result. Fortunately, the children of these races are capable of digesting lactose and, therefore, through the consumption of milk are able to obtain their proper nutrient intake during the early stages of growth and development. It is later in life that they lose the digestive ability. The same is true of cats and dogs.

More complex sugars take the form of polymers. These molecules (polymers) are made up of simple sugars that join together to form very long chains, much like the links in a long necklace made of beads as is shown in Fig. 3.1. These polymers are produced by both plants and animals to serve as storage sugars. In plants this form of sugar is known as starch. Potato starch and corn starch are sugars bound together in long chains that are formed and stored in the plants to be used as the need arises. In man this form of sugar is called glycogen and is the store of sugars in the body. The main storehouse for glycogen is in the liver and also in some of the muscle tissues.

A polymer sugar which man cannot digest is cellulose, the structural component of grass, wood, and many vegetables. Cellulose is also composed of a long chain of simple sugars. However, the linkage between the simple sugars in these chains is made in such a way that it cannot be broken down by man and, therefore, cannot be digested and utilized for energy.

Many animals, such as cows, have special mechanisms in their digestive tract for dealing with cellulose. The cow chews grass during the initial intake, swallows it, and the grass is deposited in an "extra stomach." There special bacteria work on it with a special chemical to break it down into digestable compounds. The partially decomposed substance (the cud) is then regurgitated into the cow's mouth, rechewed, swallowed, and eventually digested. The relationship between the microorganisms in the cow's body that assist in the digestive process and the animal's digestive process is known as symbiosis. The same is true for the termite. The termite cannot digest wood, but the bacteria in his mouth can, and thus supply food for the maintenance of the insect.

The Use of Sugars in the Body

Sugar is a source of energy. As stated earlier, it supplies the body with 4 Cal per gm. The energy derived from sugars is used to carry on many different processes. Muscle movement is a very important use of the energy derived from sugar. For the most part, sugar is the only nutrient that is utilized for supplying energy for muscle movement. In addition, the burning of sugar for muscle movement creates heat that is useful for maintaining body temperature. This energy is pro-

duced by a complex reaction of the sugar with oxygen in the
body. This produces carbon dioxide and water as waste products. The carbon dioxide is exhaled and some of the water is
passed out of the body by urination and perspiration. The process is represented by the following equation: Glucose + $6O_2$
$\rightarrow 6CO_2 + 6H_2O$ + heat + energy.

The Biochemistry of Sugar Breakdown

The process of breaking down sugar is a very complex chemical reaction which is represented in a very simplified form in
Fig. 3.2. Once sugar enters a cell it goes to special sites.
There it is decomposed by one of two different methods, depending upon the quantity of oxygen available in the cell. The
presence of oxygen in the cell is necessary for the breakdown
or *burning* of the sugar. Normally, an adequate supply of
oxygen is available for this burning process and as a result
sugar breaks down to an acid and two molecules of a special
compound called ATP. ATP is a large molecule containing
phosphorus and this molecule is the most important product
of the metabolism of sugar. ATP is the most energy-rich
compound in the body and is found at all subcellular levels
where energy is required. It is the chemical that supplies the
energy by the process of losing phosphorus.

When sugar is burned under normal conditions, initially
pyruvic acid and two molecules of ATP are formed. From
this point additional energy is produced when the acid is further
acted on. When a lot of oxygen is available to the cell, the
pyruvic acid is metabolized to form carbon dioxide, water,
and an additional 36 ATP molecules. This breakdown process
is known as the Krebs Cycle. Sugar has the overall potential
of producing 38 ATP molecules by going through the Krebs
Cycle, which provides a large amount of available energy
for growth, repair, and maintenance.

One of the major facets of this complex breakdown process
is the fact that each step requires the presence of an enzyme
or coenzyme in order for the reaction within each step to
occur. The presence of the enzymes or coenzymes is necessary because a chemical barrier has to be overcome in order
to initiate the reactions required. The chemical state of the
body at normal temperature cannot *kick -on* these reactions.

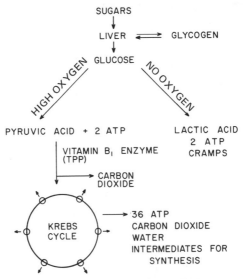

FIG. 3.2. METABOLIC PATHWAY FOR ENERGY PRODUCTION

However, the enzymes, which are protein molecules, act as catalysts to push the reaction along while the body maintains normal temperature. These reactions yielding energy for the body can therefore take place at a temperature where they would normally not occur. This is one example of the body's high degree of efficiency.

Within these reactions the functions of some of the vitamins that we require become evident. The reaction which initially breaks down pyruvic acid into the Krebs Cycle requires the presence of a special vitamin-enzyme complex, thiamine-pyrophosphate (TPP). Vitamin B_1 (thiamine) is a major component of TPP. Similarly, other reactions occurring within the Krebs Cycle require the presence of other B vitamins, some of which serve many different functions.

Acids, such as those found in the Krebs Cycle, are also utilized for food processing. For example, citric acid, one of the chemicals produced in the breakdown of pyruvic acid, is used for controlling the acid level (pH) in foods. Succinic acid, fumaric acid, and oxaloacetic acid, which are other Krebs Cycle acids, are used in the processing of foods. Food labels indicate the presence of these acids in the form of additives in many instances. However, in normal metabolism

these acids are converted into carbon dioxide so that the
bloodstream is basic in nature, not acid.

The Krebs Cycle is also important as the point of origin
for many of the other chemical pathways that occur in the
body. The steps within the Krebs Cycle are starting points
for the synthesis of the chemicals required for many of the
body's functions, such as the production of building blocks
for proteins.

As indicated before, high oxygen levels in the blood and
tissues are necessary for the complete breakdown of sugar.
There are instances, however, when an adequate supply of
oxygen does not exist. Over-exercise depletes the muscles
of their oxygen supply. In this situation, the sugars do not
break down into pyruvic acid as a starting point for the initiation of further energy-producing reactions in the Krebs Cycle;
instead, the reaction stops at the breakdown point, where
lactic acid is formed. Lactic acid causes high acidity in the
muscles and yields only 2 ATP's. Not only is this process
inefficient, since only 2 ATP's are formed, but the acid builds
up and causes cramps. Cramps are the result of this biochemical reaction produced when the muscles are overstressed
in the absence of an adequate supply of oxygen.

Control of Sugar Metabolism

When sugar is digested it goes from the intestine into the
bloodstream and directly into the liver. Within the liver it
is converted to body starch (glycogen) and is stored there
until it is needed. When the muscles require energy the sugar
in glycogen is reconverted into glucose which can then be
utilized by the muscles for contraction. The steps by which
this occurs are very complex and require the presence of
some of the hormones. For example, when we become ex-
cited, a hormone produced in the brain goes to the adrenal
glands and causes them to release the hormone adrenalin.
Adrenalin is a chemical that turns on the enzymes of the liver
to effect the breakdown of glycogen into glucose. The glucose
level in the blood then increases and is distributed among
the various tissues of the body. The glucose cannot enter
the tissues until another reaction occurs. A certain portion
of the pancreas, stimulated by the increase of glucose levels

in the bloodstream, secretes insulin (another hormone) into the bloodstream. This hormone somehow enables the glucose to enter the cells where it can be metabolized to provide the energy for the necessary functions of the cells.

Diabetes is a condition resulting from the failure of the pancreas to provide an adequate supply of insulin. In this state a person can have high levels of sugar in the bloodstream after a meal but the cells cannot take in the sugar to produce energy. Subsequently, under extreme conditions a diabetic can go into a coma and shock unless there is an alternative source of energy. Body fat can serve as this alternative source, so a diabetic person who does not have an adequate supply of insulin will break down his own body fat.

Diabetics are able to utilize sugar to the extent that an intake of too much sugar will cause the liver to convert the sugar into triglycerides, a form of fat. Fat cells are the major storehouse of energy-rich triglycerides. In quantity, this storehouse greatly surpasses glycogen storage. In a normal person this conversion of sugar to fat also occurs if too much is eaten. In other words, we require so many calories for our body functions. If we overeat, the body, rather than burning the fat, sugar, or protein to provide energy, will store the excess as fat tissue. In this way calories do not serve as a supply of energy for immediate use; they count, however, in that the body does not excrete the excess but rather converts it into unwanted fat deposits.

Another problem in the conversion of sugar to energy can also occur. Obesity in older people somehow leads to damage of the insulin-secreting tissues of the pancreas, and a mild form of diabetes occurs. Obese people cannot control their output of insulin and therefore health problems as described above occur. This type of failure may be attributed to the fact that many people go on crash diets or return to eating heavily; the consequence of these extreme eating behaviors is damage to the insulin-producing and control mechanisms. One should be very careful about going on fad diets.

Another disease related to carbohydrate metabolism is a deficiency in vitamin B_1. As stated previously, vitamin B_1 is necessary for the breakdown of pyruvic acid for the commencement of reactions in the Krebs Cycle. This is an enzymatic process, and without vitamin B_1 the consequent Krebs

Cycle reactions are not possible. More important, the total amount of ATP produced equals 36 in this reaction, so if vitamin B_1 is absent there is an extreme lack of energy-rich material. In vitamin B_1 deficiency, tremors are the first clinical symptoms that appear. This condition, known as polyneuritis, results from the inability of the nerves to function properly. There is not enough energy for proper nerve transmission and hence tremors develop which can eventually lead to a state of paralysis. This disease is common in some parts of the world.

Quick-Energy Food

Quick-energy foods should also be discussed at this point. A few years ago several liquid products were put on the market and advertised as a potential source of quick energy. However, under the conditions of normal digestion it takes from 2 to 3 hr for food to go through the digestive tract into the small intestine where it can be broken down and absorbed by the body. Therefore, in reality, quick-energy foods do not exist, since it takes several hours for absorption to occur. Some nutritionists believe that the results some people report are actually psychological.

The philosophy behind these drinks was based on the fact that they were composed of sugar in the form of glucose, which is the major sugar required by the body. The remaining ingredients in the drink were composed of salts that are similar to those found in the bloodstream. The basis for use of these products was the assumption that if the solution was similar to the composition of the blood, the sugar would be quickly absorbed through the lining of the digestive tract before it progressed to the small intestine, thereby reducing the digestion time period and thus producing quick energy. This has not been proved to be effective, and, in fact, recent works have indicated it is not true. Some people feel that eating a candy bar gives them extra energy. This may be possible, but as stated, it usually takes 2 to 3 hr for food to be absorbed into the bloodstream. Most likely, eating under these circumstances stimulates the adrenal glands to break down the stored glycogen, or else the extra energy comes from the breakdown of the stored triglycerides in the body.

TABLE 3.1
ALCOHOLIC BEVERAGES
Caloric Values and Alcoholic Content of Portions Commonly Used

Liquor	Measure (Approx.)	Weight (Gm)	Cal	Carbohydrates (Gm)	Alcohol (Gm)
Distilled liquors					
Liqueurs					
Anisette	1 cordial glass	20	75	7.0	7.0
Apricot brandy	1 cordial glass	20	65	6.0	6.0
Benedictine	1 cordial glass	20	70	6.6	6.6
Creme de menthe	1 cordial glass	20	67	6.0	7.0
Curacao	1 cordial glass	20	55	6.0	6.0
Brandy	1 brandy glass	30	73		10.5
Gin, dry	1 jigger, 1½ oz	45	105		15.1
Rum	1 jigger, 1½ oz	45	105		15.1
Whiskey, rye	1 jigger, 1½ oz	45	119		17.2
Whiskey, scotch	1 jigger, 1½ oz	45	105		15.1
Wines					
California, red	1 wine glass	100	85		10.0
California, sauterne	1 wine glass	100	85	4.0	10.5
Champagne, domestic	1 wine glass	120	85	3.0	11.0
Madeira	1 wine glass	100	105	1.0	15.0
Muscatel or port	1 wine glass	100	158	14.0	15.0
Sherry, dry, domestic	1 wine glass	60	85	4.8	9.0
Vermouth, French	1 wine glass	100	105	1.0	15.0
Vermouth, Italian	1 wine glass	100	167	12.0	18.0
Malt liquors (American)					
Ale, mild	8 oz	230	100	8.0	8.9
Ale, mild	1 bottle, 12 oz	345	148	12.0	13.1
Beer	8 oz	240	114	10.6	8.9
Beer	1 bottle, 12 oz	360	175	15.8	13.3
Cocktails					
Daiquiri	1 cocktail glass	100	125	5.2	15.1
Egg nog (Christmas)	4 oz. punch cup	123	335	18.0	15.0
Gin rickey	1 glass, 8 oz	120	150	1.3	21.0
High ball	1 glass, 8 oz	240	165		24.0
Manhattan	1 cocktail glass	100	165	7.9	19.2
Martini	1 cocktail glass	100	140	0.3	18.5
Mint julep	1 glass, 10 oz	300	212	2.7	29.2
Old Fashioned	1 glass, 4 oz	100	180	3.5	24.0
Planter's Punch	1 glass, 4 oz	100	175	7.9	21.5
Rum sour	1 glass, 4 oz	100	165		21.5
Tom Collins	1 glass, 10 oz	300	180	9.0	21.5

Muscle Differences

A genetic difference between various kinds of muscle tissue
has recently been discovered which is an interesting factor

relating to energy consumption. For instance, both a pheasant
that flies short distances, and a goose that may migrate 2000
miles before landing must break down sugars and fats to produce the energy they need. Both need a lot of ATP, but they
need it at different rates. It has been determined that there
is a genetic difference in the physiology of the different muscle
tissues that is the basis for the utilization of energy at different
rates. The long-distance flyer, like a long-distance runner, has
higher glycogen levels in the muscle fibers, and the muscle
fibers produce ATP at a slow, constant rate. The energy is
produced at a slower rate, allowing an adequate supply of
energy over long time periods. The short-distance flyer, like
a weight lifter, needs short bursts of energy. Weight lifters and
pheasants have what is called fast muscle fibers. These fibers
produce a lot of ATP very rapidly. It is also consumed very
rapidly to enable them to use more energy in a shorter period
of time.

Alcohol

Another form of food energy is alcohol which is not a true
carbohydrate. Alcohol produces 7 Cal per gm and is absorbed
very rapidly. In fact, it can be absorbed in the mouth, the
esophagus, and the stomach. Some people consume up to
10 to 20% of their calories as alcohol, usually at the expense
of carbohydrates and fats. Table 3.1 lists the caloric value
of some common drinks. Alcohol consumption is only a problem
when it occurs in excess. High concentrations in the bloodstream affect the brain and nervous system. This occurs
when the metabolic system is overloaded and the alcohol cannot be broken down any faster. Alcohol can also affect the liver
and cause it to lose some of its functions. Many alcoholics
suffer from tremors that are directly related to the insufficient
consumption of B vitamins. The lack of vitamin B causes a
lower ATP production which results in these tremors. One
should moderate alcohol intake in order to prevent these
problems.

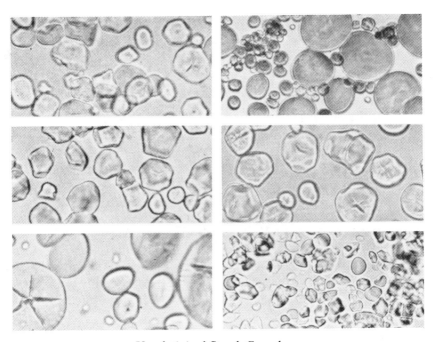

Ungelatinized Starch Granules
Upper: Left, corn; right, wheat.
Center: Left, waxy corn; right, grain sorghum.
Lower: Left, rye; right, oats.
Magnification 500X

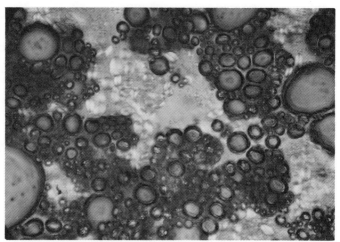

Photomicrograph of Compound Emulsion Showing Fat
Encircling Air Bubbles and the Fat Suspended in a
Continuous Water Phase.

CHAPTER 4

Fats

Composition of Fats

Just slightly less than half of the calories in the diet of the average American are derived from the various types of fats. Fats are complicated molecules containing a greater amount of carbon and hydrogen than found in carbohydrates. Because of this, fats provide more energy, approximately 9 Cal per gm, compared to 4 Cal per gm for carbohydrates.

Figure 4.1 shows the structural appearance of a triglyceride, which is the normal fat molecule found in tissues. It can be compared to a tuning fork. The presence of 3 fatty acids in conjunction with glycerol produces the normal triglyceride. Triglycerides serve as the major storehouse of fats in the human body as well as in animal tissue.

The inner portion of the triglyceride fat molecule is composed of a molecule of glycerol, which is a breakdown product of glucose in the pathway to pyruvic acid. Connected to the glycerol are the fatty acids, which are the sources of high energy levels. The fatty acids are arranged in long chains of hydrogen and carbon connected together, yielding a molecule that requires a large amount of oxygen in order to burn. Therefore, when used in the body, fats produce a substantial amount of energy.

Figure 4.1 also shows two other kinds of fat molecules found in the body in much lower levels. The compound known as a monoglyceride has only one fatty acid connected to the glycerol; a diglyceride has two fatty acids on the glycerol molecule. Labels of many foods like salad dressings and breads indicate the presence of monoglycerides and diglycerides as food additives. They are used because these molecules possess the unusual property of being able to stabilize foams and emulsions. This is due to their structure.

Kinds of Fats

The fatty acids that are important in the functioning of the human body are separated into two kinds of fats—saturated

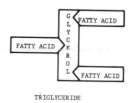

TRIGLYCERIDE

DIGLYCERIDE   MONOGLYCERIDE

FIG. 4.1. STRUCTURE OF FATS

and unsaturated. The saturated fats are those which usually appear to be solid at room temperature. The fat layers seen in meats are examples of saturated fats. They don't melt unless they are heated on a stove or in an oven. The saturated fat most common in animal tissue is stearic acid. It has 18 carbons, as the structure in Fig. 4.2 shows.

Food tissues have very diverse forms of these saturated fats, increasing in carbon number in some instances and decreasing in carbon number in others. For example, Fig. 4.2 shows the structure of the 16-carbon palmitic acid, which comes from palm oil. Also shown is butyric acid. This fatty acid is found in butter and only has 4 carbons. One form of rancidity in foods occurs when butyric acid is broken off from the normal triglycerides. In the free form butyric acid produces a bad odor, making the butter unacceptable.

The other classification of fats is unsaturated fats, which are usually liquid at room temperature. Most of the fats of vegetable oils are unsaturated. That is why salad oils are liquid at room temperature. Chemically, unsaturated fats differ from saturated fats by the presence of double bonds in the structure. These bonds make the fat more susceptible to oxidative breakdown, an undesirable chemical reaction with oxygen that occurs in the body as well as in foods. A

Saturated Fats

Stearic Acid — CH_3 CH_2 CH_2 CH_2 CH_2 CH_2 CH_2 CH_2 CH_2 CH_2 CH_2 CH_2 CH_2 CH_2 CH_2 CH_2 CH_2 COOH
Palmitic Acid — CH_3 CH_2 CH_2 CH_2 CH_2 CH_2 CH_2 CH_2 CH_3 CH_2 CH_2 CH_2 CH_2 CH_2 CH_2 COOH
Butyric Acid — CH_3 CH_2 CH_2 COOH

Unsaturated Fats

Oleic Acid — CH_3 CH_2 CH_2 CH_2 CH_2 CH_2 CH_2 CH_2 CH$=$CH CH_2 CH_2 CH_2 CH_2 CH_2 CH_2 CH_2 COOH
Linoleic Acid — CH_3 CH_2 CH_2 CH_2 CH_2 CH$=$CH—CH_2—CH$=$CH—CH_2 CH_2 CH_2 CH_2 CH_2 CH_2 CH_2 COOH
Linolenic Acid — CH_3 CH_2—CH$=$CH—CH_2—CH$=$CH—CH_2—CH$=$CH—CH_2 CH_2 CH_2 CH_2 CH_2 CH_2 CH_2 COOH

FIG. 4.2. CHEMICAL COMPOSITION OF VARIOUS FATS

double bond is a place in the molecule where a hydrogen is missing on two adjacent carbons. This double bond stimulates the oxidative process.

Differences among the unsaturated fats are based on the number of double bonds present. Those fats having only a single double bond are known as monounsaturated fats. Oleic acid is a monounsaturated fat found in olive oil (see Fig. 4.2 for chemical composition). It differs from stearic acid only by the double bond. Oleic acid is not required by the body because the body is able to create it from the breakdown products of sugars and other fats. The polyunsaturates are those fatty acids containing two or more double bonds. Polyunsaturated fats are very susceptible to breakdown in the presence of oxygen.

Liquid salad oils, such as corn oil, cottonseed oil, and soy bean oil, are for the most part polyunsaturated. Butter is a relatively saturated fat containing stearic acid and is thus a solid at room temperature. The production of solid vegetable shortenings or margarine requires the hydrogenation of liquid oils. This process adds hydrogens to the missing places. Through manipulation of this process, various textures of margarine may be achieved and a more stable fat is formed.

Linoleic acid, also shown in Fig. 4.2, is an example of a polyunsaturated fat with two double bonds. The intake of linoleic acid is required since it is the one fat that cannot be manufactured by the body. Linoleic acid is found in high concentrations in vegetable oils and to a smaller extent in meats. Linoleic acid is the basis for the building of all the structural elements of fats in the body and is, therefore, one of the *essential nutrients* required by the body. Some fish have fats that have many double bonds (like linolenic acid in Fig. 4.2), and thus fish oils are very unstable.

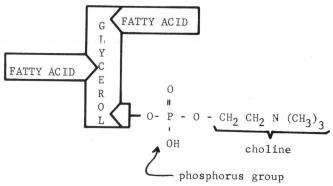

FIG. 4.3. STRUCTURE OF LECITHIN

Other fats that are very important in the metabolism of the
body are the phospholipids, which are similar to the diglycerides. The phospholipids are located at energy sites within the
cell and function in the transfer of energy. They contain phosphorus (hence the name) and an alcohol, as well as two fatty
acids. The composition of these two fatty acids can vary
greatly. Lecithin is one of the phospholipids that is manufactured by the body. It is shown in Fig. 4.3. Lecithin and
other phospholipids are involved in the production of hormones
as well as in other metabolic processes. Lecithin occurs in
high concentrations in eggs and soy beans. It is extracted for
use in salad dressing and cake mixes because it helps to impart stability to the emulsion. The presence of lecithin is
one reason eggs can be beaten into a foam. It functions even
better than mono- or di-glycerides.

The last major form of fat in the diet is sterol. Cholesterol
is an example and will be discussed in the next chapter.

Fat Metabolism

When fats are metabolized to energy in the body they also
follow a pathway that enters into the Krebs Cycle. However, a
dangerous condition can exist if fats become the major source
of calories, that is, when carbohydrates drop below 10% of the
calories in a diet. In this case, there are not enough chemicals in the Krebs Cycle to draw in the fat metabolites and
break them down. Thus intermediate chemicals build up in

the blood. These intermediate chemicals are acids and ketones. One example is acetone, the same chemical used in nail-polish remover. If the level gets too high, the acids and ketones affect the brain and a person can start having hallucinations and eventually may go into a coma. This has occurred with people who go on severe starvation diets. If a person stays in an acidosis or ketotic state (acids and ketones from the fat breakdown in the blood and urine) for a long time, the kidneys are overtaxed. The kidneys try to excrete these compounds to maintain a balance in the blood. Over-exertion can lead to kidney damage.

CHAPTER 5

Fat and Heart Disease

Fats and Diseases

What is the relation between fats in the diet and disease? There is much work being done on sterols and their relation- ship to heart disease. These fats (sterols) are well known in the form of cholesterol.

The body manufactures sterols from the essential fatty acids but also takes in sterols from vegetables, meats, and other foods. There is an over-adequate supply of sterols in a normal diet of 40% fat as calories. Many researchers have linked cholesterol to heart disease. I will try to show how this link has been hypothesized.

It is a well-known fact that Americans have doubled their consumption of meat during the last 20 years. Today Americans are consuming meat at a rate of 180 lb per person per year. During the last 20 years, the incidence of the many types of coronary diseases has also risen. Approximately *1,000,000* deaths a year have been found to be due to heart attacks or some other form of heart disease. Therefore, this fact has furnished one of the links between animal fat and heart disease. Animal fat contains more cholesterol than plant fats, and for this reason cholesterol is sometimes linked to heart disease. However, consumption of saturated fats has also increased as a result of their presence in meat. Thus some researchers have attributed the link between heart disease and fats to saturated fats instead of cholesterol.

It is known that in arterial disease there are blockages in the arteries known as plaques, which are growths or masses of chemical products deposited on the walls of the artery. These blockages narrow the space that the blood flows through, forcing blood pressure to build up. The tissues of the walls may then become weak and the high blood pressure will cause them to burst. This is what causes hemorrhaging. Analysis of the plaque indicates the composition to be cholesterol, proteins, minerals, and saturated fats. For this reason, many re- searchers have concluded that cholesterol and saturated fats

in the diet are the main culprit. Usually, people suffering
from blood clots or plaque build-up have high levels of fat
and cholesterol in their blood, indicating high levels of intake.
These high levels then cause the plaques to form.

Other researchers attribute heart disease to high sugar
intake. Consumption of sugar (sucrose), however, has remained relatively constant for the last 70 years (110 to 120 lb
per person per year). A change has taken place in our intake
of sugar in that we are now consuming less of the polymeric
forms of sugars, that is, we eat less starches. Dr. Yudkin
at the University of London feels that this trend should be
reversed.

Evidence of hypertension is also on the increase. Hypertension is synonymous with high blood pressure and can be
attributed to intake of high levels of salt. When salt enters
the bloodstream, to protect the body from its effects, water
is excreted from the cells to reduce the concentration. Thus
the capillary system has to pump more water. This causes
the heart to overwork and could cause rupture of a blood
vessel.

Others attribute heart disease to smoking and to the general
conflicts and stresses of every-day life. These conflicting
data and interrelationships make it difficult to link a single
factor to heart disease. The fact remains, however, that 60%
of all deaths in the United States are due to coronary or vascular disease, i.e., heart attacks, brain hemorrhages, or
hemorrhages of arteries. In addition to 600,000 people dying
each year from coronary heart diseases, another 1 million
people have a mild form of heart attack each year. The chances
of people continuing to live after experiencing a heart attack
are about 5 times less than for those who have not experienced
heart failure. Another 200,000 deaths are due to some form
of arterial disease. These are extremely serious statistics.

Cancer of some form accounts for another 20% of all deaths.
As we will see in a later chapter this disease may also be related to diet.

Diet and Heart Disease

Why is diet held accountable for these statistics? There are
many who would blame cholesterol and saturated fats, as we

have seen. It is true that the average American diet has
changed and that heart disease has increased, but are these two
related or are they merely coincidence? We eat more meats
and, therefore, more cholesterol and saturated fats than before. Tests for measurements of blood cholesterol levels
made all over the world indicate that people in other areas
of the world have much lower cholesterol levels and fewer
instances of heart disease than those in the United States.
There is not as yet enough research to prove conclusively
that fats cause heart disease. In fact, as we will see, recent
research seems to be pointing in the other direction.

One of the reasons more people die of heart problems today
than 20 years ago may simply be that modern medicine has
practically conquered infectious diseases such as tuberculosis,
smallpox, cholera, malaria, and typhoid fever that used to
kill thousands every year. Infant mortality is now extremely
low, but was quite high 20 years ago and is still high today
in the underdeveloped nations. People in the United States
today have better incomes and can afford better medical care
than the last generation. In short, the rise in the statistics
for heart disease may be partly attributed to the fact that
the general population of the United States is living long enough
today to die from heart disease, cancer, and other diseases
of old age.

How was proof of the relationship between diet and heart
disease determined? One sizable experiment known as the
Framingham Study was conducted over a period of close to
20 years in Framingham, Massachusetts, in an attempt to
correlate this relationship. In an attempt to relate the results to heart disease, scientists observed the diets and life
styles of 40,000 people. From this study there was some
evidence that those who experienced heart attacks had higher
levels of cholesterol in their blood. The evidence was not
absolutely clear-cut. Several years ago the study was termi-
nated due to lack of government support.

Some problems existed with the ethics of the Framingham
Study because some people were consuming high-cholesterol
diets and were possibly increasing the chances of their lives
becoming a statistic on a researcher's chart. The most interesting fact that came out of the study that is not widely
known deals with the relationship between levels of cholesterol

in food and levels of cholesterol in the body. The study showed
that to lower the level of cholesterol in the blood by 3 mg per
liter, the amount of cholesterol in food consumed must be
lowered by 100 mg. Therefore, in reality, it is very difficult
to change the levels of cholesterol in the blood by diet restriction. It is possible that some people with severely high levels
of cholesterol in the blood and indications of heart disease
can reduce levels by the sharp restriction of the intake of
cholesterol in their diet, and thus possibly increase their
chances of survival. However, on the average only small
changes result, and diet restriction may be meaningless.

The American Heart Association advises the necessity of a
drastic reduction in the intake of foods that are high in cholesterol. The AHA claims that foods high in cholesterol such as
eggs and meat as well as saturated fats should be avoided.
They should be replaced with an increased intake of margarine
and vegetable oils instead of butter and animal fat for cooking
and for spreading. It is recommended that beef be replaced
with chicken and fish because of their lower levels of saturated
fats.

Recommendations of the American Heart Association include
reducing the intake of fats to less than 35% of total calories
consumed. Many people at the present time have as much as
45 to 50% of their total caloric intake in the form of fats. As
mentioned, consumption of polyunsaturated fats instead of
the saturated fats is advised. Consumption of polyunsaturates
could lead to a problem unless there is a concomitant increase
in the intake of vitamin E. The association between vitamin E
and polyunsaturates will be discussed later.

Since it is not positively known that cholesterol is the only
link between the diet and heart disease, the American Heart
Association has also suggested that the intake of sugars be
lowered, and that sugars should be consumed in their more
complex forms, that is, as starches. In addition, lowering
of dietary salt intake is also advised. All these seem advisable
to some degree.

The Food and Drug Administration has recently made allowances for the labeling of cholesterol content in foods, but no
limits of cholesterol in the diet have been set.

An opposite point of view in relationship to the intake of increased amounts of polyunsaturates can also be a point of

concern. Studies in which rats were fed very high levels of
polyunsaturates showed evidence of premature aging. One
of the theories for this aging process is based on the fact
that polyunsaturates are very susceptible to reaction with
oxygen. The combination of polyunsaturates and oxygen yields
a compound that is highly reactive with proteins and causes
the protein to become insoluble. This can cause toughening
in foods. The studies show that the animals fed a large amount
of unsaturates do not have shorter life spans, but their physical
appearance shows premature aging characteristics. Adding high
levels of vitamin E to the diet seems to prevent this.

The Scientific Controversy

Following are some quotes from prominent scientists about
the correlation between cholesterol and heart disease. Dr.
Michael DeBakey, who discovered many new techniques for
studying heart problems, performing heart surgery and making
heart transplants, states: ''We found very little relationship
between diet, cholesterol level, and coronary artery disease.
Much to the chagrin of many of my colleagues who believe
in this polyunsaturated fat and cholesterol business, we have
put outpatients on no dietary program, no anti-cholesterol
medications. We have found that 80% of our patients with
severe occlusive coronary artery disease had had blood cholesterol levels comparable to the levels in normal people. When
the levels are comparable, it doesn't make sense that elevated
cholesterol levels are the cause of coronary artery disease.''
(Comments at the Cardiovascular Disease Seminar, Dandiger
Institute of Menorah Medical Center, Kansas City, Missouri,
1971.)

Dr. R. Reiser of Texas A & M states, "High cholesterol
levels among young people could be due to starting life with
too little cholesterol in their diets." It is possible that there
is too little cholesterol available in the diet of infants because
of the use of synthetic formulas instead of mother's milk.
Thus during the first few years of growth and development
the body would establish mechanisms to over-produce the
needed cholesterol. These mechanisms would then stay in
effect during the remainder of one's life, providing unneces-
sarily high levels of cholesterol. Conversely, if infants are

fed high levels of cholesterol in their early diets, the body would not initiate the development of mechanisms that would produce large amounts of cholesterol at later stages of life. Studies substantiating this theory have been done with rats, but once again the ethical problem of doing such studies on humans arises.

Dr. Philip White, Director of Nutrition for the American Medical Association, concluded, "I don't think anybody really knows and the burden of proof is on those who make the allegations. The main confusion relates to the promotional methods used by the American Heart Association. Apparently, the Association firmly believes that the present mode of life leads to early death and that by making certain changes in diet and exercise, the risk can be significantly reduced. We are all tired by now of the unending advertisements for oils and margarines that promise to clear out arteries in much the same way a drain cleaner works in a sink." ("Chaos in the Cracker Barrel," Speech at Food Editor's Conference, Honolulu, February 5, 1971.)

In 1970, G. V. Mann said, "The Framingham data are consistent with all other careful studies—diet practice and the behavior of coronary heart disease have not been causally related. Scattered cross-cultural studies and results with bizarre experimental diets fed to a few research subjects have been consistently misinterpreted. The error is one which every student of logic is warned about—the reductive fallacy—a single simple cause is given to a complex effect." . . . "Physicians who have tried diet therapy for high levels of blood cholesterol and coronary heart disease soon find that it doesn't work. Diet therapy is indeed an impotent treatment of hypercholesterolemia, and no one has shown it to be an effective preventive for coronary heart disease". . . "Diet fat has only a modest corrective effect, of academic rather than practical value. Until the biochemical lesion is identified and corrected, the best recourse is regular exercise and maintained physical fitness, which seem to negate the vascular impairment." ("Diet and the Framingham Study," Letter to the Editor, Medical World News, October 9, 1971.)

Overall, a distinct controversy exists between the effect of cholesterol in the diet on heart disease. Warnings made by the American Heart Association indicating the exclusion of beef and pork from the diet, eating only one egg per week, and using margarine instead of butter, if followed, may create other serious health problems. Until all the facts are known about this very complex issue, a positive stand cannot be taken. Regular exercise and a moderate, well-balanced diet are all that can be recommended at this point. This is supported by other studies of groups of men who consume high levels of dietary saturated fat and cholesterol, but who in addition do a moderate amount of exercise or work under conditions that require high physical activity. Perhaps this exercise also tends to reduce mental stress which may cause imbalances and also lead to coronary disease.

CHAPTER 6

Protein

An Instance of Protein Nutritional Effects

There are many misconceptions about nutrition in existence today. One of the most popular concerns the effects of protein on man. Many people, especially some vegetarians, feel that the proteins from meat cause one to become aggressive. This misconception can be traced back to an experiment conducted at the London Zoo in the early 1800's. The London Zoo was having problems with some overly noisy and aggressive bears. It was decided to try an experiment to see if a change in diet would quiet the bears down. They had been fed raw meat as the major part of their usual diet. In order to establish the effects of the meat on the animals, bread was substituted for the meat. As a result, the bears became extremely docile and lethargic. As we will see, they became docile because they did not get a balanced diet and were too malnourished to have enough energy to be aggressive. This experiment was regarded as definitive proof that meat protein caused aggression and was eventually published in a scientific journal! It was regarded by many as an established fact for quite some time.

Functions of Protein

There are several reasons why both bears and man need protein and become lethargic without it. (1) Protein is needed by the body to build and repair tissues. The tissues of the body are constantly undergoing breakdown and change, and new protein components are required on a continuous basis to resupply the repair process with building blocks to take the place of those that have been used up or excreted. (2) The body needs enzymes for the initiation of the many chemical reactions in the body. Protein is the major component in the structure of many of these enzymes. (3) Protein also serves as an energy source if there is a lack of fats and carbohydrates

45

in the diet. Excess protein, on the other hand, will be converted and deposited in the form of fat to be used later as a supply of energy.

Composition of Proteins

Proteins, like carbohydrates, are made up of molecules linked together in long chains with many thousands of units in each chain. The individual units are called amino acids and are the building blocks of protein. There is a much greater variety in proteins than in carbohydrates. Besides linking together in different numbers and with different bonds, as do carbohydrates, there are over twenty-two different kinds of amino acids that have been identified as constituents of proteins. The possibilities for producing different proteins are almost limitless with this many amino acids combining in any assortment and in any number. These amino acids form different sequences for each protein, the sequence determining the shape and function of the individual protein. For example, silk proteins are straight, flat chains; hemoglobin has a ball-like appearance; and casein, a milk protein, has different size chains held together by the mineral calcium in a very complex arrangement. Many other proteins are composed of several chains wound around each other in a spiral arrangement called a helix. Some of these helixes have extremely complicated structures.

Essential Amino Acids.—Of the known amino acids, only 8 are absolutely required by the adult human body. These are listed in Table 6.1. Recent evidence has shown that histidine, another amino acid, may be required. The remaining amino acids can be manufactured from the 8 essential amino acids and carbohydrates and fats. Protein in the diet serves as the major source of nitrogen for the body and is, therefore, necessary for the production of the amino acids, since carbohydrates and fats only supply carbon, hydrogen, and oxygen.

There are various qualities of protein found in foods. If a protein has all the essential amino acids in the right balance it is a high-quality protein. A poor-quality protein may be low in one or more of the essential amino acids. Flour is very low in lysine content and thus is a source of poor-quality

TABLE 6.1
ESSENTIAL AMINO ACIDS

Isoleucine
Leucine
Lysine
Methionine
Phenylalanine
Threonine
Tryptophan
Valine
Histidine (may be required)
Arginine (infants only)

protein. The body cannot use this protein efficiently. This was the problem for the bears in the London Zoo experiment.

Tryptophan, another essential amino acid, is significant on a world-wide scale because corn is low in tryptophan. Corn serves as a major part of the diet in many countries. Because it is also low in lysine it is a very poor quality protein source. The areas that use corn as the basis of the diet have suffered major malnutrition problems. Through genetic manipulation researchers at Purdue University have recently developed a strain of corn, Opaque-2, that is high in lysine and tryptophan. Seemingly, it would have been the answer to the problems of malnutrition in South America and Mexico where corn is a major part of the diet. However, due to growing conditions unsuitable for Opaque-2, the corn's poor resistance to pests, and the sociological response to the new yellow corn instead of the old white corn, Opaque-2 did not enjoy as much success as originally anticipated. Work is being done to make it more acceptable in these areas.

Another interesting essential amino acid is phenylalanine. Phenylalanine can be used to point out genetic errors of metabolism. Frequently, people are born without certain enzyme systems in their body so they cannot properly metabolize certain chemical components of the foods they eat. One example, phenylketonuria (PKU), is a disease that affects a number of infants each year who do not have the ability to break down phenylalanine. This amino acid will build up to toxic levels in the blood, and a high concentration in the brain will cause severe brain damage. Tests have been developed which can be administered at birth, or even before, to determine if the child has PKU. If the child does have this condition he is placed on a diet that is extremely low in phenylalanine to prevent brain damage. After 5 or 6 years many of these children can adjust to a normal diet.

Protein Quality of Foods

A good-quality protein is one that contains all the essential amino acids in a proper balance. This balance is usually defined using eggs as the point of reference. The amino acid composition of eggs constitutes a high-protein quality of 100% because eggs have the essential amino acids in the balance closest to that required by man. All other foods can be compared to eggs to determine their respective protein qualities. Protein qualities for various foods are shown in Table 6.2.

Milk and meat have qualities based on protein scores of about 80%. Cereals are around 40 to 70% quality. This means that cereals cannot be utilized as readily as eggs and meat for growth and maintenance functions. It is possible to improve the protein quality of cereals by adding lysine to white flour or cereal products, thereby upgrading the quality of the protein. Gelatin is one of the poorest of proteins since it contains no tryptophan and, contrary to popular belief, eating gelatin does not make nails grow. In fact, the protein in nails is keratin which is entirely different from the protein in gelatin. Keratin contains a lot of methionine, which gelatin lacks. Only balanced nutrition, care, and a little luck will help.

Rice, a major food source in the world, is also a poor-quality protein with only a 72% quality score. Rice has caused much the same nutritional deficiency problems as corn. One way the protein quality of the diet may be upgraded is to mix two proteins, for example, milk on cereal or mixing soy protein with meat. This way the deficiency of one protein is countered by the other.

Protein quality as measured by the PER (Protein Efficiency

TABLE 6.2
PROTEIN QUALITY VALUES

Food	Protein Score[1]	Biological Value Growing Rat	Adult Human
Egg	100	87	94, 97
Milk (cow's)	78	90	62, 79, 100
Casein	80	69	70
Beef	83	76	67, 80, 84, 75
Fish	80	75	94
Oats	79	66	89
Rice	72	—	67
Corn meal	42	54	24
White flour	47	52	42, 40, 45, 67, 70
Wheat germ	61	75	89
Soy flour	73	75	65, 71, 81
Potato	56	71	80, 71, 81
Peas	58	48	56, 90
Cassava	22	—	—

[1]Based on a comparison to eggs.

Ratio) is a better test, as it involves an actual feeding study, not just a comparison of composition. This test utilizes rats that have been just weaned from their mother. They are fed for 28 days on a test diet containing the protein being studied as 10% of the total diet. Weight gain versus time is measured and is compared to a control diet in which casein from milk is the protein. Weight gain divided by the amount of protein fed yields the protein efficiency ratio. This is adjusted to the value of casein for comparison. Since weight gain is also affected by the total diet and not just by the intake of protein, many interpretation problems exist with this type of measurement. However, PER is usually used since it is easy to do compared to other animal-feeding studies. The PER value usually follows the protein score in terms of protein quality.

Nitrogen Balance and Biological Value

Most of the dietary nitrogen is acquired by intake of protein and is excreted as urea. The amount of nitrogen taken in minus the amount of nitrogen excreted should indicate the amount of nitrogen accumulated in the body. A protein quality test called nitrogen balance uses this technique. Nitrogen levels in the food are measured, feces are collected daily, urine is collected, and nitrogen losses through hair and skin are also calculated. If a high-quality protein is being fed in the proper amount the nitrogen balance (intake minus output) will equal zero for an adult in maintenance. This indicates that the protein (the essential amino acids) is being consumed in amounts necessary for maintenance and growth of cells. If a negative nitrogen balance occurs (intake lower than output) this can indicate an intake of either too little protein or of poor-quality protein. In this condition muscle tissues are usually broken down to supply the necessary essential amino acids. A person in this state would lose muscle mass. A positive nitrogen balance means that nitrogen is being incorporated into the body by the growth of new tissues. One would find this in growing children. This unfortunately also occurs in tumor growth or cancer.

Another measure for determining protein quality is called Biological Value. This measurement is usually made in a growing animal and is the amount of protein or nitrogen that is retained by the body divided by the amount of protein digested. It is one of the best methods for comparing protein qualities; however, it is very difficult to do. In addition, studies cannot be ethically used on growing children or pregnant women. Table 6.2 lists some biological values for various proteins. As can be seen, the numbers vary quite a bit for the same protein. This is an inherent problem when comparing human studies done at different places, and is the reason the controversy exists over nutritional requirements, especially for protein. In most cases in Table 6.2 all three quality indices are similar.

Protein Requirements

Based on PER studies and additional biochemical studies, the protein requirements for man have been established. The average requirement set by the National Research Council recommends the intake of 40 to 55 gm of protein per day for the average person; 25 to 30 gm of the total protein RDA should be consumed in the form of high-quality protein, such as meat, milk, and eggs. The rest can be consumed as rice, bread, corn, etc. Balancing these various protein sources serves to provide the body with all the essential amino acids. In terms of mg/kg of body weight, growing children require about 3 times as much protein per lb of body weight.

Further studies indicate that it is possible to live on only 25 to 30 gm of high-quality protein per day. Some of this work has been done with people who have lost their kidney function and are undergoing dialysis. These people require a lower intake of protein because of the inability of the kidneys to remove the breakdown products from an excessive intake. If they eat too much protein the nitrogen breakdown products can cause nausea, vomiting, and shock. An interesting factor is that if only the essential amino acids are fed by mouth, the kidney dialysis patients metabolize the food normally. However, if the 8 essential amino acids are fed intravenously, an additional amino acid, histidine, is required to maintain health. The reason for this is not known. In infants and possibly growing children all 10 amino acids in Table 6.1 are required, but at maturity only the 8 at the top are required for maintenance levels.

Protein Consumption Problems

Around the world protein supplies vary. In the Orient, where the major portion of the diet consists of rice, 20 to 30 gm of low-quality protein are consumed in an average day. Since rice is only 2 to $2\frac{1}{2}\%$ protein, about 5 lb of rice would have to be consumed in a day to meet an RDA of 50 gm. Actually Orientals do consume over 2 lb of rice per day; however, as stated, this protein has poor quality and must be supplemented with beans and nuts. Many do not do this and thus live on the borderline of protein malnutrition. Of course, there have been suggestions that the RDA is set too high.

Problems also exist with consuming too much protein. In the United States the average adult consumes up to 100 gm of protein per day. For a person with normal kidney function this is no problem. Protein breakdown products eventually form ammonia and then urea. The liver converts the ammonia to urea to maintain the acid-base balance in the blood. The urea can be utilized for other metabolic functions such as making the non-essential amino acids. However, most of it is excreted in the urine. If the kidneys fail, the build-up of high levels of urea in the bloodstream occurs and a condition known as uremia results, which causes nervous disorders, upset stomach, and toxic conditions that can lead to death. People with kidney failure require routine removal (2 to 3 times weekly through dialysis) of the toxic substances in order to survive.

The maximum protein requirement for man is not known. Athletes who are building new muscle tissues and constantly repairing them sometimes eat over 250 to 300 gm of protein per day. People on a maintenance diet utilize protein primarily to maintain nitrogen balance in the body; that is, they take in just the amount needed for repair and maintenance of the cell functions. The over-consumption of protein by athletes is meaningless. If an athlete wants to add on 20 lb of muscle tissue in one month, he need consume only 4 extra lb of protein; the other 16 lb of the muscle tissue is water. Because of this, 60 gm per day over the RDA is all that is needed. This means about 90 to 110 gm per day rather than the 250 to 300 gm actually consumed. Several extra glasses of milk and an extra serving of meat at breakfast should be enough. Any extra protein consumed will go into calorie requirements of the exercise, or will be turned into fat. A weight gain greater than 20 lb per month is probably dangerous.

Intolerance

An intolerance for certain sugars such as lactose, which was discussed in Chapter 3, can result in a disease. Likewise, intolerance for certain proteins can also cause diseases. One of these is celiac disease, an intolerance for gluten, the protein found in wheat. It does not show up until growing babies begin eating bread and start losing weight instead of gaining. Diarrhea is the main sympton. This disease affects about 1 in every 8000 births to some degree. If bread is eaten it cannot be digested because the intestinal wall is affected. Most of the food eaten is then passed directly into the feces without absorption. Loss of weight occurs as other tissues break down to supply the required calories and nutrients. This disease can be helped very easily by removal of gluten from the diet. Wheat flour that does not contain this gluten protein is produced commercially. In many cases, this condition disappears after a few years. In others, the disease may be so mild that it goes unrecognized until late in life when it shows up again. In later life it is usually called non-tropical sprue.

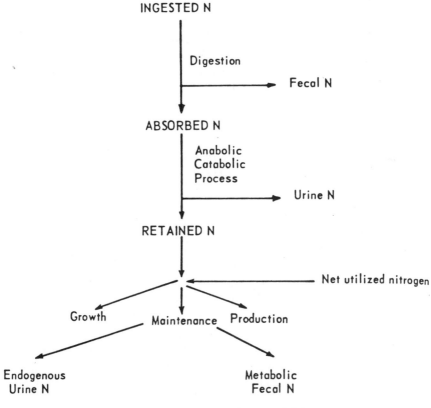

Food Protein Nitrogen Utilization Scheme

CHAPTER 7

Water and Oxygen

Oxygen

Oxygen is probably the most essential nutrient. We don't recognize it as such since it is not eaten but involuntarily con-sumed in the process of respiration. If the oxygen supply were eliminated, we would die in a few minutes. Oxygen is necessary for the burning of sugars, fats, and proteins in the body, as was discussed earlier, to produce ATP. Therefore, oxygen can be considered an essential nutrient required by the body, since we could not survive without it.

Ironically, we possess a very inefficient mechanism for the utilization of the oxygen we breath into our lungs. Close to 3300 gal. of air a day are taken in, and from that air less than 10% of the oxygen is utilized. The rest is exhaled with the carbon dioxide in the breath.

Water

Water comprises about 60% of the human body. Though less vital than oxygen, it is still extremely essential. A human can survive approximately 4 days without water. Water is con-sumed in several ways. Primarily, it is obtained by drinking and eating foods in a level equal to approximately 3 pt (1500 cc) per day. The water we get in foods comes to about 750 cc, and the metabolic water (the water that forms when sugar, fat, and protein are burned) is another 350 cc. Output of water by respiration is about 40 cc per day; by perspiration through the skin, on the average, about 500 cc; by excretion in the urine about 1700 cc; and in the feces 150 cc per day.

Overall, the intake of water should equal the output of water. During many diseases a condition called edema occurs in which water is retained by the body. This is usually seen first as a swelling of the limbs. This condition is extremely dangerous if prolonged, since it usually indicates a salt imbalance. Drugs can be used to decrease edema but the original disease should be treated instead. Protein deficiency also causes edema. In some cases, the mothers of children with severe protein mal-

nutrition (Kwashiorkor) feel that their children are all right
since they are not skinny. Size is not always a good indicator
of physical condition, as was mentioned earlier.

Extra water consumption is extremely necessary for people
who go on a high-protein or high-fat diet. In a high-protein
diet, such as the consumption of large amounts of meat and
eggs, there is a simultaneous consumption of large amounts of
fats. Utilizing this fat for energy produces great quantities of
ketones, as discussed earlier. Without a high water intake to
flush them out of the bloodstream, one could reach the state of
ketosis and go into a coma. High-protein or high-fat diets are
thus not recommended.

A person should normally consume at least $1\frac{1}{2}$ to 2 qt of water
per day. Diets which recommend the intake of lesser amounts
of water are dangerous to the kidneys because chemicals become concentrated in the body with the potential to cause severe
reactions.

CHAPTER 8

The Micronutrients—Vitamins

Kinds of Vitamins

It has only been during the last 60 years that most of the vitamins have been discovered and isolated. Prior to that time, from about 1860 to 1910, most scientists were looking for germs or bacteria as the cause for diseases which were ac- tually due to nutritional deficiencies. Pasteur's discovery of disease-causing microbes was largely responsible for the belief that all illnesses prevalent at that time were due to microorganisms growing in the body. This search for bacteria hindered the probe into the nature and functions of the vitamins.

Vitamins are utilized in special pathways to assist chemical reactions while the body maintains normal temperature. There are two categories of vitamins, the water-soluble vitamins and the fat-soluble vitamins. This nomenclature is based on the way in which they are isolated, and does not mean that they function only in water or in fat. When the amount of a fat- soluble vitamin is measured in a food, for example, the food is extracted with an organic solvent which takes out the vita- min and the fat. It can then be measured after separating it from the solvent and fat. Water-soluble vitamins are usually extracted with a salt-water solution. It is interesting to note that any excess intake of water-soluble vitamins is usually excreted rapidly in the urine, while an excess intake of fat- soluble vitamins is stored in the body fat tissues for later use.

Water-soluble Vitamins

Vitamin B_1 — Vitamin B_1 (thiamin) is one of the water- soluble vitamins. A lack of vitamin B_1 in the diet produces a disease that was evident as early as 2600 B.C. and was re- ferred to as beriberi ("I cannot" in Chinese). The disease causes muscular weakness and leads to polyneuritis which is a form of paralysis. In adults it prevents movement of the limbs and in children it causes retardation of growth.

The disease was located primarily in the Orient where people had a diet composed primarily of polished rice. The polishing of rice was an ancient practice which served as a method for cleaning rice. In many parts of the Orient people felt that brown rice was dirty and, therefore, polished rice was much more desirable. Beriberi became very prevalent in the 1700's and 1800's as improved techniques for polishing rice were invented which resulted in the removal of even greater amounts of thiamin. A rice kernel contains a bran around the outside and the primary location of the thiamin is within the bran. Rubbing the rice between stones to polish it breaks the bran off and removes the brown color leaving an attractive white rice. At the same time the thiamin is lost.

In the 1800's the Japanese were losing great numbers of sailors due to their rice diets. Dr. Takaki, a Japanese doctor who had worked in the British Navy, decided to experiment to see if these losses could be reduced. Two ships were sent out with 276 men on board each ship. On one ship the traditional Japanese white rice diet was utilized, but on the other ship he administered the British Navy diet which consisted of meat, milk, eggs, and rice. At the end of 9 months almost 200 of the 276 men on the rice diet had developed beriberi. On the other ship only 14 people developed the disease. Interestingly, these 14 people did not like the British diet. They had smuggled their own familiar supply of white rice on board and were not eating the British diet. Unfortunately, the Japanese doctor did not realize the relationship between white rice and beriberi and instead attributed the malady to a germ present in the white rice. At the same time the thiamin is lost.

Dr. Eijkman, a Dutch physician, went to an Indonesian hospital in 1886 to study beriberi. He noticed that chickens brought to the grounds for the purpose of supplying eggs gradually developed the symptoms of beriberi. He observed this for about 3 months, after which the chickens suddenly recovered. Eijkman discovered that the camp had changed cooks after the 3-month period and that the new cook was feeding the chickens brown rice, or peasant's rice. The cook felt he could not feed the more expensive white rice to the chickens. Based on this observation, Dr. Eijkman concluded that there was a disease organism in white rice and searched for it unsuccessfully. However, he was successful in getting people to eat brown rice to cure the disease.

In 1911 Casimir Funk, a Polish scientist, extracted about 800 lb of the bran hulls from rice and after isolation, produced 6 oz of a white powder. This powder came to be known as thiamin. He originally classified it as vitalamine, a nomenclature he invented, but this was later changed to vitamin.

Basically, vitamin B_1 is found in meats, liver, whole grain cereals, and inactivated dry yeast. Some foods have a factor which destroys vitamin B_1. People have acquired vitamin B_1 deficiencies by eating raw clams and raw fish as a continuous part of their diet. Within the raw oysters or raw clams there is a chemical which destroys thiamin. Some people, due to a genetic factor, maintain a condition in the body which con-sistently breaks down thiamin, and a deficiency will be prev-alent throughout their lives if this condition is not treated. The instances of this disease, however, are rare.

When foods are cooked and processed, some thiamin is lost because it is sensitive to heat. Today rice is enriched, or par-boiled. This process can be traced back to the times when the Indonesians, Chinese, and Japanese all had beriberi but the Indians did not. The Indians had developed a process for easier removal of the hull by parboiling the rice. The rice was placed in boiling water for a while, then taken out and dried. This allowed the hulls to break off more easily when ground. When the rice was placed in boiling water, the water caused the vita-mins to penetrate into the interior of the rice, allowing a major part of the vitamin to remain in the rice. At the present time most commercially processed white rice is handled in a similar manner. High-pressure steam is used to force large amounts of thiamin into the rice kernel. Some white rice contains higher percentages of thiamin than does brown rice because of this processing method, and also because extra thiamin is sometimes added.

Cases of beriberi are almost non-existent at the present time in the United States but do occur occasionally in other parts of the world. A well-balanced diet prevents thiamin deficiency. The RDA for thiamin was shown in Table 2.1. As stated previously, thiamin is necessary in the conversion of sugars into the Krebs Cycle where ATP is made. This is why a thiamin deficiency leads to nervous disorders: not enough ATP is being made to supply the energy needs of the body for muscular movement or nerve transmission.

Niacin.—Niacin (nicotinic acid) is another water-soluble vitamin. Pellagra, the disease caused by lack of niacin, is still very common in various parts of the world, especially in Africa. The word pellagra means *rough skin*. Parts of the body exposed to the sun suffer from a severe reaction; the exposed area becomes covered with lesions that are very red and very rough. A smooth, red tongue also accompanies this disease. Niacin deficiency causes diarrhea and may eventually lead to mental instability due to lack of ATP. Niacin functions in much the same manner as thiamine. It is necessary in the breakdown of sugars to form ATP. However, its lack does not completely stop manufacture of energy as in the case of thiamine.

Niacin deficiency did not become prevalent in the United States until it appeared in the South during the Civil War. People who developed this disease subsisted largely on diets of corn with very little milk.

The germ theory was studied as being responsible for pellagra, but it was found that feeding milk or meat in very small quantities could prevent or cure this disease. A cup of milk fed daily was enough to cure it. For about 70 years scientists were looking for the chemical in milk that cured pellagra. They never found it. Niacin is not present in milk, but tryptophan, one of the essential amino acids that make up proteins, is present. Under conditions in which low levels of niacin are present in the diet, tryptophan can be converted into niacin in the body. Tryptophan is, therefore, a provitamin, a chemical which can be converted into a vitamin within the body. Niacin was not isolated until 1937, when its importance was discovered. The widespread use of milk in this country today has prevented pellagra.

Vitamin C.—Another water-soluble vitamin whose deficiency is no longer common is vitamin C (ascorbic acid). The disease that results from a deficiency of vitamin C is scurvy. As mentioned previously, the failure of early sea explorers to carry along a balanced diet led to the death of many seamen. This in turn probably slowed down the discovery of the New World. In those times scurvy was thought to be caused by the cold, damp weather on board ship. Analysis of the records kept revealed that the seamen consumed diets basically composed of dried beans, cheese, and some salted, dried beef. There were

no fruits or vegetables for the common sailors, yet the officers
always had a supply of these foods. The officers were much
less prone to scurvy. However, the dietary factor was not
associated with the disease until much later.

Symptoms of vitamin C deficiency are lesions in the mouth,
weak and bleeding gums, and finally, loss of the teeth. Occasionally scurvy still shows up in the United States. Dentists
sometimes treat gum problems as periodontal disease when
it is actually scurvy. The most amazing fact about scurvy is
that in advanced stages it causes old wounds to reopen. James
Cook, the famous explorer, wrote about some of his sailors in
their late 60's who had 50-year-old wounds reopen. This factor
can occur because vitamin C is extremely instrumental in the
formation of strong tissue bonds. It is involved in the chemical
crosslinking of tissue proteins so that they can be held together.

James Lind, a British medical officer and one of the first
men to discover the effects of vitamin C, noticed the difference
between the diets of the officers on board ship and the common
sailors. In 1710 he ran an experiment on one of the ships he
was assigned to where he fed the sailors a variety of diets. He
fed some of the sailors two oranges a day, which cured their
scurvy, whereas the other tested diets had no fruits and those
men retained the disease. Upon his return to London, Lind
went before the Royal Medical Society and presented the results
of his experiments and was laughed at for the simplicity of the
results. No one believed that a disease could be so easily cured
by a change in diet.

The British Navy forbade Lind to continue these experiments
on other ships. It was not until 1795 that the British Navy concluded that the results of Lind's experiments were accurate.
They then added liquid lemon juice to the diets of the sailors.
At that time, lemons were called limes, and the British sailors
receiving the daily dose of lemon juice became known as *limeys*.

The British Navy was the only fleet that recognized the importance of fruits in the diet. The mission of Adamson Scott,
who went to the North Pole in 1912, ended in death for everyone
because there were no canned or fresh fruits and vegetables in
the diets of his explorers. Autopsies of the men revealed that
they all had scurvy.

Scurvy is not fatal in itself but the presence of the disease
lowers the body's resistance to other diseases which eventually

prove to be fatal. The real relationship of vitamin C to diseases caused by low resistance is not known. It was not until 1932 that the chemical which comprises vitamin C, ascorbic acid, was isolated and identified by Albert Szent-Györgyi at the Mayo Clinic in Rochester, Minnesota, and Dr. Charles G. King of the University of Pittsburgh.

Vitamin C is found mostly in fruits and vegetables and is the least stable of all the vitamins. Heat-processing such as the overcooking of vegetables can result in a 30 to 50% loss of vitamin C. Raw vegetables have higher levels of vitamin C. The industrial canning of peas, for example, destroys about 20% of the vitamin C. When added to the amount destroyed in meal preparation, the consumer can end up with less than one-half of the original vitamin content.

In addition to the importance of vitamin C in tissue formation, many people also believe vitamin C helps to prevent stress caused by disease. Linus Pauling, who won the Nobel Prize in Chemistry and the Nobel Peace Prize, wrote a book on using vitamin C as a preventive for the common cold, but conclusive evidence supporting this has yet to be uncovered. A 1974 study conducted by the University of Toronto Medical School utilized a double blind experiment. A double blind experiment is one in which the doctors who administer the doses and who check the patients do not know if the subjects in the experiment are receiving a placebo (something that looks, tastes, and smells like the drug but has no effect) or the test drug. Only the researcher who sets up the experiment is aware of the dosages and who is getting what. In this experiment involving about 2000 students there was no significant difference in the number of colds contracted, but there was a 40% reduction in the duration of colds for people who were given vitamin C. For example, instead of having a cold for 3 days, it may have only lasted $1\frac{1}{2}$ days.

One problem with taking too much vitamin C occurs with people who have gout. Gout is caused by the overabundance and deposition of the breakdown products of some of the large molecules which form the genetic material in cells. These molecules are known as RNA and DNA. Uric acid is one of the products formed when DNA decomposes. Under certain conditions where the blood chemistry changes, deposition of uric acid in the joints of the body can occur. One of the first joints to be affected is the big toe. Gout is sometimes apparent in

men, appearing at 30 to 35 years of age as a sudden pain in a
big toe lasting for a very short time. A tendency toward gout
can be made acute by an excess intake of vitamin C, which
can change the acidity of the blood. At high vitamin C levels,
uric acid crystals will deposit in joints, leading to severe pain.
The medical profession believes about 5% of the male population
of the United States has a tendency to gout. The severity of
gout lies in the fact that these crystals can also be deposited
in the kidneys with subsequent damage to the kidneys. One thus
should be careful in taking an overabundance of vitamin C tablets.

Vitamin B_2.—Vitamin B_2 (riboflavin) is usually found in foods
wherever vitamin B_1 is present. Some people suffer from a
lack of vitamin B_2 due to genetic malfunctions and develop a
shark skin. These people have a distorted biochemistry requiring an extremely high level of B_2 that is not fulfilled. They
sometimes become carnival oddities. Riboflavin's main function is in the synthesis of ATP (energy-rich material) in the
oxidation cycle and, like thiamine, is found in meats, milk, and
liver. No real deficiencies are found in the United States.

Vitamin B_6.—Modern medicine has thus far not found a disease caused by a deficiency of vitamin B_6 for man. Adelle
Davis, a self-professed expert on nutritional disease, claims
that 50% of the people in the United States have vitamin B_6
deficiencies. This is curious since this fact has never been
published in any nutritional or medical journal. Vitamin B_6
is chiefly involved in the transformation of some essential
amino acids into the nonessential amino acids needed for maintenance. It is present in adequate quantities in most diets.

Vitamin B_{12}.—The lack of vitamin B_{12} (cobalamin) is considered to be a serious deficiency, but is not very common.
Its appearance is generally the result of an extremely unbalanced diet. The lack of vitamin B_{12} results in pernicious
anemia. This vitamin works in the formation of the hemoglobin
in the blood. Hemoglobin is responsible for carrying oxygen
in the blood. Low levels of vitamin B_{12} lead to the failure of
hemoglobin to form, and thus an adequate supply of oxygen cannot be provided to the cell membranes where energy is being
produced. Consequently, this causes a reduction in the formation of ATP since the oxygen is needed to burn glucose. Thus a
loss of energy ensues. Vitamin B_{12} is found in almost all foods

except fruits and vegetables. Vegetarians may exhibit the anemic conditions caused by a B_{12} deficiency after a period of 3 to 5 years if they had consumed meat in their diets prior to becoming a vegetarian. This is because B_{12} is partially stored in the body and is used only slowly. Vitamin B_{12} is the only B vitamin that is stored; the others are utilized continuously, or if an excess is consumed, they are excreted. Prior to the invention of a synthetic vitamin B_{12}, it had to be extracted from calves' liver. Over one ton of liver was required to produce an amount equal to the weight of less than 1/3 of a penny. Today it is readily available for therapeutic use.

Other B Vitamins.—Folic acid, lipolic acid, biotin, and pantothenic acid are all B vitamins which are present in foods. These vitamins have not shown to be deficient in human diets, although Table 2.1 lists an RDA for folic acid. It has not been conclusively determined whether the body can manufacture these 4 vitamins. Biotin, it is believed, may be produced by bacteria in the large intestine and then absorbed into the body. In any case, the diets of Americans are not deficient in these vitamins and the Food and Drug Administration will not allow companies to make any unwarranted therapeutic claims for them.

Fat-soluble Vitamins

Two of the fat-soluble vitamins, A and D, are important historically because of the worldwide prevalence of diseases caused by deficiencies of these vitamins. The other two fat-soluble vitamins, E and K, rarely produce a nutritional disease in humans.

Vitamin A.—Vitamin A (carotene) is basically associated with the eyes. For centuries many children, especially children in the Orient, became blind because of a deficiency in vitamin A. In World War I the Danes sold all the butter they manufactured to England in order to earn money for armaments. Consequently, children at that time were forced to drink skim milk. Since the butter fat had been removed and vitamin A remained in the fat, many of them became blind due to a lack of the vitamin. Vitamin A is one of the chemicals necessary in the sensing mechanism of the eye that helps convert light into messages to the brain. The early manifestation of vitamin A deficiency is night blindness, a condition in which a person is not able to adjust to darkness. Eventually if no vitamin A is supplied, the eyes become scaled over and the person becomes totally blind.

It was not until the 1930's that vitamin A was isolated from butter fat and from green leafy vegetables. Butter fat contains vitamin A and the green leafy vegetables contain provitamin A, a form which is converted into vitamin A in our normal meta-bolic pathways. Vitamin A is also found in eggs and fish liver. Interestingly, polar bear liver is extremely high in vitamin A. Eskimos are very fond of liver, but have learned that polar bear liver should be excluded from their diet, because the extremely high levels of vitamin A it contains can cause death. Vitamin A in excess can cause toxicity problems because it is stored in the body. In 1960–64, about 20 children in New York died be-cause mothers thought if 1 tablet of vitamin A was good, then 2 tablets were better and gave overdoses. These children were getting vitamin A in their milk, butter, and vitamin tablets. Hypervitaminosis developed and led to death. The symptoms of hypervitaminosis from vitamin A are yellowing and peeling of the skin, fragile bones and finally, extreme liver damage. The RDA for vitamin A is shown in Table 2.1. Many people take in less than this because they don't eat vegetables or liver and may experience some very minor form of deficiency. A change in diet is all that is necessary to correct this.

Vitamin D.—Vitamin D deficiency, rickets, did not show up until the 1600's and 1700's in Europe when people migrated to the cities and began living in slums. People dwelling in the slums lived with high levels of smog caused by the burning of wood and coal. This eventually cut down the levels of sunlight (a source of vitamin D) available to these people in overcrowded areas.

Rickets usually affects children and causes malformation (bowing) of the legs. This is because vitamin D (ergosterol) is very important in the absorption of calcium from the intestine. If insufficient vitamin D is present in the diet not enough cal-cium is absorbed and the bones cannot form properly.

The early study of rickets led to many controversies. The Scots who lived in small towns usually did not contract rickets. They attributed this to the fact that they drank cod-liver oil every week. Medical people again could not believe something

as simple as fish oil could cure the disease. The issue was
also complicated by the fact that people living in the slums in
the Orient did not exhibit signs of rickets. This was later
attributed to the fact that they received much more sunlight
than did the Europeans. It was not until 1922 that vitamin D
was isolated from cod-liver oil. At the same time it was discovered that sterols, like cholesterol present in the fat just
below the skin, were converted to vitamin D upon exposure to
sunlight.

Another important factor concerning vitamin D is its ability
to be stored in the body fat. As seen in Table 2.1, adults do
not need vitamin D. This is because they have acquired an adequate supply by the age of 25. The body can extract vitamin D
from the fat tissues when needed. Taking in an excess of vitamin D does not cause death but can cause symptoms of continuous diarrhea and a calcification of the kidneys.

Vitamin D is found in the butter fat of milk, in meat fats, and
in fish-liver oils. Most milk has vitamin D added to it, as does
margarine, to serve as a factor of safety. Dry milk which has
had the fat removed is required by law to have vitamin D added,
since this form of milk has become an important part of many
diets.

Vitamin E.—There are no known deficiency diseases in man
caused by a lack of vitamin E (tocopherol). The RDA shown in
Table 2.1 has been set at what is found in a normal diet, not by
research, because it is impossible to create a human deficiency,
although it can be produced in some animals. Rats fed diets
with no vegetable oils exhibit high rates of stillborn births,
males become sterile, and the blood breaks apart (hemolysis);
however, none of this has occurred in people on low vegetable
fat diets.

Some doctors have made many wild claims for the virtue of
vitamin E to the extent that massive doses heal burns, cure
arthritis, and improve sexual prowess. However, these claims
have never been proved. The only claim that is substantiated is
that vitamin E does seem to retard the aging process by preventing unsaturated fats from breaking down. If the body fats
are decomposed, substances produced can destroy tissues. Vitamin E prevents or slows this process, at least in studies with
rats.

Toxicity from an excess of vitamin E has not been shown in

humans to date, although in chickens, liver damage has been shown. Adequate supply of vitamin E can be obtained by con-suming vegetable oils such as cottonseed, soybean and corn oils as well as whole-grain cereals.

Vitamin K.—Vitamin K has not been shown to be deficient in man; however, it is not present in foods. It is one of the very few vitamins that are produced by bacteria in the large intestine and can be absorbed into the body through the intestinal wall. Vitamin K is important in the formation of blood clots. A de-ficiency occurs only when massive doses of antibiotics are given. The intestinal bacteria are completely destroyed by the antibiotic and vitamin K cannot be produced. Hemorrhaging may take place, but this condition rarely occurs, and is known well enough so that the patients are given vitamin K.

CHAPTER 9

Minerals and Trace Elements

Other Essential Elements

The nutritional significance of many trace elements is an area which is only being discovered today. This points out again the infancy of nutrition as a science. In this chapter several essential elements will be discussed from the standpoint of (1) their distribution in the body and in foods, (2) their function, and (3) the daily requirements. Some are required in large amounts, for example, the calcium requirement is about 0.8 gm per day, whereas an average person needs less than 1/10,000 of that level for iodine, which is also considered an essential element. Very few trace elements have been found to be essential. Most of those that are essential work as co-factors with the myriad of enzymes in the metabolic process. Deficiencies which show easily recognizable symptoms are rarely encountered in the United States. However, the real question today is whether the increased consumption of fabricated and refined foods in which the trace element concentrations have possibly been reduced or altered will eventually lead to disease problems. This possibility fortunately seems remote right now because of the extremely small amounts required. The only deficiencies that have been found involve the elements that have greater requirements, such as calcium.

Sodium and Potassium.—These two elements are found in almost all foods and are important in maintaining electrical and chemical balance between the tissue cells and the blood. Sodium somehow remains outside the cells in the bathing fluid while potassium is located inside the cell wall. When a muscle undergoes contraction or an impulse travels along a nerve, there is a rapid exchange of these two elements across the cell membrane. How or why this occurs is unknown but the exchange creates the electrical impulse.

There are no RDA's for either sodium or potassium. However, the excessive intake of table salt (sodium chloride) has been implicated in coronary heart disease and in hypertension (high blood pressure). In the latter case, the reason for elevated blood pressure is the fact that salt retains water in the body. Salt is found mainly in the blood; as salt intake increases, the blood volume increases with more water to keep the concentration level. Thus the heart has to pump harder to move the extra blood. Many doctors and nutritionists suggest that people cut down on salt intake, substituting potassium chloride for sodium chloride when possible. Those with kidney disease or kidney failure have to eliminate salts altogether, since they cannot pass urine, which is the only way salt is removed. The high levels of salt in the body would then cause very high blood volumes. The potassium-sodium balance could then be upset, which could lead to congestive heart failure.

An average person in the United States consumes from 3 to 6 gm of sodium per day. The intake of potassium is a little less (2 to 5 gm per day). Astronauts in space need more potassium because in the absence of gravity it tends to leak out of cells and is excreted. This is taken care of by supplementing their diet with potassium. Most animal foods contain higher amounts of sodium than potassium whereas the reverse is true of vegetable foods.

Calcium and Phosphorus.—Like sodium and potassium, the roles of calcium and phosphorus are closely related. These two elements comprise 70% of the mineral weight of the body, being found mainly in the bones and teeth as special mineral salts. The RDA's are shown in Table 2.1, each being about 0.8 gm/day for adults.

The ratio of calcium to phosphorus in the bones is about 2:1. This suggests that intake through food should be about the same ratio. Contrary to popular opinion, the bone is an active tissue. The calcium, once deposited as a part of the bone, doesn't remain there forever. If calcium is needed somewhere else in the body, it can be redissolved from the bone, transported and used. For example, calcium is necessary in the process of muscle contraction, in maintaining the acid-base balance of the blood, as an activator of many enzymes and as part of the formation of protein complexes such as in the clotting of blood. Phosphorus is important in the structure of phospholipids and especially in the formation of ATP and other energy-rich components in the body cells.

The rate of exchange of calcium and phosphorus is about 1% per day between bones and tissues even in the adult. As noted earlier, this exchange is controlled by vitamin D. If enough vitamin D is not present in the diet of children they will have poor bone formation and develop rickets. In addition, the blood has to maintain about a 2:1 ratio of calcium to phosphorus. If one or the other gets too high the bone is depleted in order to compensate. Also without a 2:1 ratio in the food during digestion, calcium absorption is decreased.

Unfortunately, due to a decrease in the consumption of milk and other dairy products, the average American dietary calcium-to-phosphorus intake ratio is in many cases less than 1:1 or may even be 0.5:1. This is further exacerbated by the fact that the phosphorus level in many processed foods (e.g., soft drinks and hams) is high because phosphorus is used to retain water, give the food a juicier texture, or create an acid taste. After the age of 30, if not enough calcium is consumed, the bones slowly become depleted especially because of high phosphorus intake. The resulting disease is called osteoporosis. It is very prevalent in old age when the bones have become thinner, shorter, and are brittle and weak. Osteoporosis could be prevented by an increased consumption of calcium and maintenance of that consumption. Unfortunately, very few foods have high calcium-to-phosphorus ratios. Most of them, like seaweed, whole fish flour, and alfalfa, are not liked or readily available. Dairy products are currently the best source. The food industry is and should be taking steps in this area to supplement processed foods with calcium and to reduce the amount of phosphorus used.

Magnesium.—Magnesium is the last major mineral found in the body. Its distribution is similar to that of phosphorus, about 70% in the skeleton and 30% in the tissues. The RDA is shown in Table 2.1.

A magnesium deficiency is rarely found because magnesium is present in all foods. It is highest in cereals and vegetables. In the latter it is the green pigment chlorophyl. Two or three servings of bread and vegetables a day supplies all the needs of the body. The only reported deficiencies have been found in children who have been fed strictly on a milk diet, since milk is low in magnesium.

Magnesium is required in muscle contraction as well as being a co-factor of the many enzyme systems that take part in the Krebs Cycle and in nerve transmission. A deficient diet causes

hyper-irritability. In extreme cases a form of tetany (the
cessation of muscular movement—a condition much like lock-
jaw) takes place and the person dies since breathing is no
longer possible. This is rare, but has been found in cattle
who were fed magnesium-deficient grass.

Trace Elements

Iron.—Iron is one of the most important trace minerals in the
diet. In Table 2.1 one can see that the RDA is much greater
for children and women than for men. Also it can be seen
that it is required in much smaller amounts than the other
minerals listed. On the average the need is only 0.01 to 0.02
gm per day which is less than 1/1000 oz.

The main function of iron is in the formation of hemoglobin,
the chemical that carries oxygen in the blood. This oxygen is
needed in the cells to burn glucose so that energy and heat
can be produced. Some iron is also found in the liver where it
is mainly stored for later use. This is why animal livers are
such a good source of iron.

Anemia is one of the most prevalent forms of nutritional
diseases in the United States. If enough iron is not consumed,
the number of red blood cells which contain the hemoglobin is
reduced, and thus not enough oxygen can be brought to the
cells. A person in this condition becomes lethargic. Iron
deficiency can be caused by too low an intake in foods or by
consuming foods which prevent iron from being absorbed
from the digestive tract. Spinach, contrary to the *Popeye
image*, contains oxalic acid, a chemical which binds iron and
prevents its absorption. Rhubarb is another food that will do
this if too much is eaten. There are also hereditary deficiencies of the absorption process.

One of the biggest problems of iron deficiency occurs with
women in their child-bearing years. During this time if their
monthly loss of blood through menstruation is large, they will
have a reduced hemoglobin level in the blood and can become
tired and weak. This is why the RDA in Table 2.1 is set higher
for women, to compensate for the blood loss. Women should
consume more iron-rich foods or have a doctor prescribe a
supplement if that is necessary. Many of the popular over-the-
counter iron sources are useless since the body cannot absorb

all forms of iron. Much more research is being done on the necessary forms of iron for absorption.

Iron deficiency was recognized as a big problem in the 1930's, and during World War II bread was supplemented with iron. Bread at that time was a major part of everyone's diet, so this was the easiest way to get it to those who needed it. Unfortunately, today people consume less bread and cereal products (about 20% of the diet compared to 40% previously) so iron deficiencies still exist. Recently the level of iron in bread has been increased to make up the difference, as has been recommended by the Food and Nutrition Board of the National Academy of Science.

Iodine.—In referring to Table 2.1, another essential nutrient that has an RDA listing is iodine. The daily requirement is very small, being a little more than one ten-millionth of a pound. One would expect that, as the body requirement is that low, no major nutritional deficiencies would occur. Yet in the world as a whole, *goiter*, which is a manifestation of iodine deficiency, still exists.

The chief role of iodine is in the formation of the hormone *thyroxine* in the thyroid gland. This gland is located in the neck. Thyroxine is intimately related to caloric metabolism, especially in control of the basal metabolic rate. A hyperactive person is someone who may have an overproduction of thyroxine. When iodine is deficient in the diet, the thyroid gland enlarges in order to pick up as much iodine as possible from the blood. In some parts of the world, especially in mountainous regions like the Andes and the Alps, goiter is still a serious problem. Some South American Indians, in fact, sell wooden doll souvenirs that have enlarged necks. Old art works of Europe portray subjects with goiter, as it was a common condition at that time. Today goiter can be prevented very easily by eating salt to which iodine has been added (iodized salt), or by eating ocean fish regularly. However, as not all salts are iodized and not all stores carry iodized salt, goiter is found today even in the United States. Hopefully, this will change in the future.

Other Trace Elements.—The demonstration that other trace elements are essential is extremely difficult since they are required in such small amounts. It is almost impossible to prepare a diet free of minor trace elements and then it may

not be ethical to test the diet on humans. Only recently was
zinc discovered to be a requirement through observation of
people from certain areas of the Middle East. It was found
in particular villages that there was a high incidence of dwarf-
ism. These dwarf children also did not reach sexual maturity.
Analysis of the diet showed it to be lacking in zinc and that
certain natural chemicals in the food prevented zinc absorption. Supplementation with a zinc salt reversed the symptoms
in some cases if treatment was started early enough. As seen
in Table 2.1, zinc was added to the RDA listing in 1973. The
RDA was based on a normal diet because the true requirement
is still unknown.

Cobalt, another essential trace element, is a critical component of vitamin B_{12}. Lack of cobalt will produce a type of
anemia, since this results in a reduction in vitamin B_{12} intake.
As stated previously, vitamin B_{12} is essential in the formation
of hemoglobin. A moderate intake of meat and dairy products
supplies all the needed cobalt. The problem may only occur
in strict vegetarians.

There are many more essential trace elements. Human
nutritional deficiencies from them are unknown because the
requirements are so small and so easily met. It is interesting
to note that selenium is a requirement for cattle. Lack of
selenium in certain cattle feeds has caused nutritional diseases.
Some people would like to prevent its addition to processed
foods for human consumption since selenium may induce cancer
of the liver. This points out the problem previously discussed,
namely, that an overexcess of a particular nutrient can be extremely harmful. One must learn to balance out a diet properly.

CHAPTER 10

Digestion

Pathways

The process of digestion consists of the breakdown of foods into chemicals which can in turn be absorbed into the blood. The digestion pathway is seen in Fig. 10.1. Mechanical and chemical activities in the mouth comprise the first step in digestion. The mechanical activity of chewing is important in reducing the size of food particles to facilitate later stages of digestion. The only chemical activity is due to enzymes released in the mouth from saliva. The enzymes in saliva break down large sugars into smaller chains. This is not the most important part of digestion.

The esophagus, through a squeezing action, forces food down into the stomach. No real digestion takes place here in this organ except that the salivary enzymes continue to work on the starches.

The next major area in the digestive pathway is the stomach. The basic function of the stomach is to produce acid (hydrochloric acid) and enzymes for digestion. The pH or acidity of the stomach (gastric juice) is equal to about 1.15. This makes it a very strong acid, since acidity is measured on a scale of 0 to 14 with 0 being the highest. The high acid level in the stomach is necessary for the breakdown of proteins. The enzyme, pepsin, breaks down protein into smaller pieces in the stomach, but pepsin can only function under conditions of high acidity such as are found in the stomach. Lastly, the acid in the stomach helps to separate fat into small particles which can be acted upon during later stages of digestion.

Depending upon the amount of fats taken in, food will remain in the stomach for up to 4 hr. Fluids such as soda pop can go through the stomach in less that 20 min, but a heavy, fatty meal will remain in the stomach for as long as 4 hr. This is the reason that fatty meals make a person feel full. A less fatty meal such as chop suey, composed primarily of vegetables, remains in the stomach for a much shorter time. *Quick Energy*

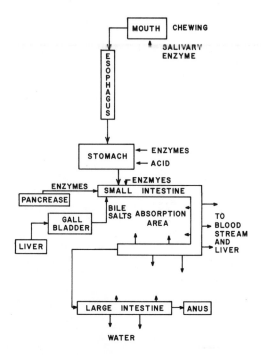

FIG. 10.1. THE DIGESTIVE TRACT

Foods also digest much quicker than a meal, but still take
longer than the claims for quick energy suggest.

The principal steps in digestion occur in the small intestine
which is separated into three sections: the duodenum, the
jejunum, and the ileum. The duodenum, which is the first
section beyond the stomach, is about 3 ft long and is the location of the major digestive processes. The food enters this
section and is immediately acted upon by bile salts. Bile salts
are produced in the liver from cholesterol and are stored in
the gall bladder until digestion begins. They help emulsify the
fats into small droplets so that they can be acted on by enzymes later. These enzymes break down the triglycerides
into the fatty acids and glycerol for absorption.

Many other enzymes go to work in the duodenum. These
originate from the intestinal wall as well as from the liver.
The pancreas also excretes some enzymes into the duodenum.
The major digestion of proteins occurs at this point. The
proteins are broken down into the single-unit amino acids

which can readily pass across the wall of the next part of
the small intestine and enter the bloodstream. The blood acts
as a transport system bringing the amino acids to the cells
of the liver. The starches are broken down in the duodenum to
form glucose, fructose, and other simple sugars which also
can be readily absorbed across the intestinal wall.

The jejunum and the ileum comprise the next 27 ft of the
intestine and are used for the absorption process. Food is
digested in the duodenum and is assimilated through the intestinal wall for use by the body in the jejunum and the ileum.
The process is very complex and is not well understood. It
is known that it is not like passing a fluid through a sieve.
The water-soluble components, such as the simple sugars,
amino acids and other chemicals, pass into the bloodstream
(portal vein) and go directly to the liver, where they are acted
on. It is here that any poisonous chemicals that are ingested
are detoxified. The fat components reassemble on the inside
of the intestinal wall into triglycerides and are transported
around the body in the lymph system.

Undigested food, as well as undigestable food such as fibrous
cellulose from lettuce, cabbage, etc., are then passed into
the large intestine which is about 4 to 5 ft long. In the large
intestine there is a high concentration of bacteria. Vitamin K,
which is produced by these bacteria in the large intestine, is
absorbed here. Some people believe that yogurt should be
consumed because the bacteria present in yogurt will accumu-
late and proliferate in the large intestine. There they will produce many desirable vitamins and nutrients. This theory has
been disproved by many clinical studies. In one particular study
(K. Acott and T. P. Labuza, 1972. Addel's Vitamin B Factory;
Food Prod. Devel.) the results showed that the stomach acid
kills 99.99% of all the yogurt bacteria. Any remaining bacteria,
as shown in other studies, could not proliferate in the small
intestine. The claims for yogurt are based on the positive
effects it has had for people who have been administered high
levels of antibiotics after surgery. The use of high amounts
of antibiotics kills off many of the organisms found in the
large intestine. In some cases doctors give large, dry pellets
of *Lactobacillus*, the organism used to make yogurt, to help
re-establish the conditions necessary for good health. Once
foods are consumed again, the other forms of bacteria present

TABLE 10.1
FOODS HIGH IN CERTAIN NUTRIENTS

Protein Foods
　　Cooked meat and poultry　　　20–30% protein
　　Fish　　　　　　　　　　　　20–30%
　　Cheese (American)　　　　　　25%
　　Cottage cheese　　　　　　　13–17%
　　Nuts　　　　　　　　　　　　16%
　　Eggs　　　　　　　　　　　　13%
　　Dry cereals　　　　　　　　　7–14%
　　Bread　　　　　　　　　　　　8%
　　Beans　　　　　　　　　　　　7–8%
　　Milk (whole)　　　　　　　　3.5%
　　Milk (skim)　　　　　　　　　4.0%
Fatty Foods
　　Oils　　　　　　　　　　　　100% fat
　　Butter and margarine　　　　80%
　　Mayonnaise　　　　　　　　　80%
　　Walnuts　　　　　　　　　　　65%
　　Chocolate　　　　　　　　　　50%
　　Peanut butter　　　　　　　　50%
　　Cheese　　　　　　　　　　　25–35%
　　Meats　　　　　　　　　　　　20–40%
　　Ice cream　　　　　　　　　　10–16%
Carbohydrate Foods
　　Sugar　　　　　　　　　　　100% carbohydrate
　　Chocolate creams　　　　　　85%
　　Cereals　　　　　　　　　　　70–80%
　　Cookies　　　　　　　　　　　70%
　　Jams　　　　　　　　　　　　70%
　　Cake　　　　　　　　　　　　60%
　　Bread　　　　　　　　　　　　50%
　　Rice, spaghetti　　　　　　　20–35%

Calcium Rich Foods　　　　　　Niacin Foods
　　Milk　　　　　　　　　　　　　Liver
　　Cheese　　　　　　　　　　　　Fish
　　Sardines　　　　　　　　　　　Poultry
　　Dark green, leafy vegetables　　Meats
　　Fish　　　　　　　　　　　　　Peanut butter
Iron Rich Foods　　　　　　　　Vitamin A Foods
　　Liver　　　　　　　　　　　　　Liver
　　Beef　　　　　　　　　　　　　Sweet potato
　　Pork　　　　　　　　　　　　　Spinach
　　Beans and peas　　　　　　　　Carrots

Iron Rich Foods
  Dark green, leafy vegetables   Cantaloupe
  Chicken   Squash
  Eggs   Dark green, leafy vegetables

Vitamin B_1 Foods   Vitamin B_2 Foods
  Pork   Liver
  Pork sausage   Poultry
  Peas   Meats
  Liver   Fish
  Veal   Cheese
  Nuts   Milk
Vitamin C Foods   Vitamin D Foods
  Citrus fruits   Fish oil
  Vegetables   Liver
  Tomato   Fortified milk
  Potato   Eggs
  Cabbage
  Liver   Vitamin E Foods
                              Vegetable oils
                              Oil seeds
                              Cereals

in the food will invariably take over the yogurt organisms
and become predominant.

The other major function of the large intestine is to reabsorb
the water that was used for digestion. This amount can be
quite large. When intestinal disorders occur, the water is not
reabsorbed and diarrhea results.

We have seen what the specific requirements for the body
are. Table 10.1 lists some of these requirements in terms
of foods that supply them. It is important to have a working
knowledge of these lists in order to balance a diet. There are
many ways to balance a diet. Many nutritionists use the basic
four, that is, eat a meal with a serving from each of 4 important groups: meats and fish; fruits and vegetables; dairy
products; and cereal products. Unfortunately, today we eat
many combination foods that don't fit into any one of the 4
categories. A pizza with sausage, cheese, and sprinkled
with onions, peppers, and mushrooms is a good example.
This pizza fits all 4 groups and is actually a well-balanced
meal if supplemented with milk, or even with wine or beer.

One should learn to look at foods this way in order to determine dietary lacks.

Remember, however, that missing one meal every now and then or eating an unbalanced meal once in a while is not going to cause nutritional deficiencies or a need for vitamin pills. In fact, one should see by now that consuming a vitamin pill instead of a meal is a very nutritionally unsound practice.

Now that we have seen what the body needs in terms of foods and what the composition of foods is, in the next chapters we will examine how processing and storage affect the nutritional value of foods.

CHAPTER 11

Some Bases for the Preservation and Processing of Foods

External Biological Hazards

One of the bases for the preservation of foods is the prevention of decay or deterioration of a food from the time of its birth or planting through slaughter or harvest until it reaches the processor. The first step in the preservation of foods is pest control. In the United States there are at least 10,000 types of insects that attack food crops. The application of insecticides can be considered a step in food preservation.

Although insects do the most damage, rats are also a problem. It is estimated that there are around 100 million rats in the United States alone. Each rat eats approximately 20 lb of food per year that was designated for human consumption and also contaminates an additional 200 lb per year, making the food unfit to eat. The combined total of food destruction by rats equals 2 billion lb per year. This destruction persists despite the availability of rodenticides and other poisons, either because these means are not used or because they are improperly used. Proper use of rodenticides could eliminate this waste of food.

In addition to pests, there are more than 1500 bacterial or viral diseases that require the use of chemical sprays as a method of protecting the plant. Unfortunately, as new plant diseases show up all the time, research must be constantly done to find new ways to prevent crop destruction. For animals, the use of good sanitary facilities, antibiotics, and the segregation of diseased animals adds to productivity. Despite all these problems, the United States has one of the best productivity rates for its agricultural products.

Decay of Foods

The desire to prevent food decay is the next major step in the initiation of processes to preserve foods. Three forms of decay occur in food: senescence, microbial decay, and chemical decay. Senescence is a form of decay that can be defined

79

as aging. Even after fruits and vegetables are picked they are
still undergoing metabolism, which causes beneficial nutrients
to be used up and destroyed. One of the objectives of food
preservation is to slow down such metabolic functions so the
food may be kept at the most beneficial nutritional state. Refrigeration is a form of food preservation which lowers the
temperature of foods enough to retard the metabolic processes
so that senescence is inhibited.

Microbial decay can occur in two forms—normal decay and
harmful decay. Normal decay organisms are those which
attack food and destroy the food such as the growth of slimy
bacteria on meat. They do not make the food injurious if consumed, although they are capable of greatly affecting the taste,
smell, and texture of food. Harmful decay is caused by the
presence of organisms which either grow on foods and produce
poisons or are poisonous themselves. Processing is used to
destroy or prevent the organisms from growing. Again, refrigeration is an example of a vehicle to slow down the growth
of some of these organisms.

Chemical decay is a form of decay in which various components of foods react to make the food poorer in quality. For
example, the fat in potato chips is composed of both saturated
and unsaturated fats. Oxygen reacting with the unsaturated
fats produces a rancid flavor which is a deterioration of the
food product. Some levels of rancidity are customary and
acceptable in many people's diets, but extreme rancidity can
lead to the production of toxic components which would render
the food inedible. A method of processing to prevent this
would be to package the chips under a vacuum, i.e., remove
the air.

Food Preservation Based on Population

Another basis for food preservation in the United States is
that our country has a geographic separation of the producer
from the consumer: 70% of the population live in metropolitan
or megalopolitan areas, while the food producers live in widely
separated farm belts. Because of this, it takes time to transport the food to the consumer. Not all foods can be shipped
rapidly enough before their decay; thus they have to be processed as quickly as possible. Because of this separation of

growers and consumers, there is a need for prevention of
the three kinds of decay discussed above (senescence, microbial decay, and chemical decay) so that the consumer can get
the highest possible nutritional value from his food. Besides
getting more nutritionally valuable foods, the consumer is
able to get out-of-season foods and exotic foods that would not
be available to him without processing because these foods
would not be able to withstand the long transportation distances.

Sociological Basis of Food Processing

Another basis for food processing is the consumers' desire
for more convenience foods in order to reduce the time required for meal preparation. We have seen many innovations
in the food industry, starting with instant foods, moving through
home-made frozen bread to frozen boil-in-the-bag vegetables
and even meals. Is the consumer really the originator of this
convenience mania? Or are the food companies responsible?
This isn't an easy question to answer. The food industry is
marketing more products at higher prices than the raw materials would cost the homemaker. The consumer, on the
other hand, needs to shop only once a week rather than every
day or two because of the preservation techniques that have
been used to prolong shelf-life. The shelf-life of bread, for
instance, has been greatly increased by the addition of mold
inhibitors that allow a loaf of bread to be successfully stored
for a week. The time for meal preparation has now been con-
siderably shortened, leaving more time for leisure activities
for the homemaker.

The consumer has also gained an increased variety of foods
because of these new innovations. The average supermarket has
approximately 8000 kinds of foods versus the 40 to 50 kinds
found in rural stores 20 years ago. The consumer is able to
have exotic foods or foreign foods without the time and effort
required to prepare them from the original, fresh ingredients.
He is also able to enjoy entirely new foods, such as special
frozen desserts, turkey rolls, and instant breakfasts that have
been "invented" by the food industry.

Many foods are consistently eaten because they have an acceptable odor, taste, texture, and color. The criteria for
judging these characteristics are largely personal and/or

cultural. To some people Limberger cheese is highly acceptable and to others it is totally undesirable. Cultural conditions
and prices allow some people to enjoy eating horsemeat, while
others cannot tolerate it. Religion also instigates the consumption of certain kinds of foods at specific times of the year.
Taste panels have proved that color is a very important factor
in the acceptability of a product. Would you like to eat green
meat?

An important basis of processing is to make sure the food
meets the desires of the consumer, whether culturally, per-
sonally, or religiously oriented. In addition, as the consumer
wants his favorite foods all year round, processing must find
a way to keep the desired quality attributes during transportation and storage.

The food industry would like to establish the fact that their
processing techniques have yielded higher-quality products.
One of the criteria for better quality is flavor. New techniques
for processing frozen foods have greatly improved this quality
factor. The nutritional quality of food is a factor that is also
gaining much attention at the present time, as it should. The
consumers have created the social and political pressure to
force processors to look at nutritional value. Processors are
doing much research and are making advances to maintain
maximum nutritional value during processing. New methods
of harvesting and freezing vegetables give frozen products
with higher flavor and nutritional quality than can be found
from fresh produce that is improperly stored.

Many food processors and food companies also want to suc-
ceed in achieving high-quality foods with respect to flavor
and odor. This means a high resale if the products are acceptable to the consumer. To achieve this, the processors
sometimes have to add certain chemicals to foods. The addition of these chemicals is a source of great social controversy
at the present time and will be discussed later. Pressure by
political and social groups can change the allowed methods of
food processing very quickly.

Historical Basis

Food-processing techniques such as freezing and sterilization are the results of the relatively new science of food tech-

nology, but processing of food products is actually an ancient practice. Some 8000 to 9000 years ago central, community bakeries were started to free the individual family from having to bake bread daily. Some of the earliest guilds or unions were formed by bakers for the purpose of sustaining their trade and improving this very important staple.

The drying and salting of foods dates back to periods of 5000 to 6000 years ago. Fermenting of foods, a chemical preservation method, is also ancient. There is a story that yogurt was discovered while men journeyed across the desert with pouches made of animal stomachs filled with milk that eventually curdled and was acted on by bacteria. Cheese is thought to have been discovered in the same way. Processing is of ancient origin but has been made a real science in order to enhance and improve the flavor and nutritional qualities of food.

Interestingly and ironically, wars have been the biggest single influence on the development of new processing techniques for foods, and many major contributions have originated from a necessity to meet war conditions. The canning of foods was discovered because of Napoleon's need for a safe food supply. Similarly, the method for making margarine was also discovered during that time.

During World War II the U.S. troops in Europe needed food in the field that could be prepared quickly. As a result, the preparation of dehydrated, or instant potatoes and eggs by new procedures was invented. The Vietnam war helped the development of the process of freeze-drying. The U.S. Army Ranger Patrols needed food supplies that could be carried in the field for long periods of time. They also needed food supplies that were nutritious, easy to prepare, and easy to carry. Freeze-dried complete dinners packaged in flexible films were the outcome.

The use of flexible film-packaged foods replacing canned foods greatly improved the mobility of troops. These innovations were given subsequent application to use in the space program and are now available to homemakers and campers. Some of these processes will be discussed with respect to nutritional value and quality. Overall, the basis of processing of foods is to: (a) make them safe for consumption at a later time; (b) maintain quality of flavor, odor, and appearance; (c) maintain nutritional value; (d) make them convenient to use.

CHAPTER 12

Microbes in Foods

Three Kinds of Microbes

There are three major kinds of microbes—organisms not usually visible to the eye—which prey on foods. They are bacteria, yeasts, and molds. Bacteria are the most prevalent and are the fastest-growing of all the microbes. Bacteria are responsible for the decay of food and the production of chemicals called toxins that are dangerous to health. Some bacteria do not produce harmful toxins but, when ingested in the body, are poisonous in themselves because of their chemical make-up. Preventing the contamination and growth of these dangerous kinds of microbes in foods is the major focal point in the processing of foods for safety.

Yeasts and molds are usually not considered to be poisonous organisms, but do cause decay of foods. Recently it was discovered that some molds produce toxins that are harmful. Yeasts, although causing some decay, are best known for their useful fermentation characteristics.

Another microscopic species, the virus, has sometimes been associated with food, although this is not common. For example, raw clams in several instances have been known to transport the hepatitis virus. The viruses themselves do not decay foods, but can be dangerous to health.

Not all organisms found in and on foods are dangerous. Fermentation, as noted, is a food process which utilizes organisms to process foods. The manufacture of bread requires yeast in order to raise the dough. Sauerkraut is produced by the fermentation of the natural organisms found in cabbage. In fact, this fermentation is an ecological balance. One type of bacteria grows and produces an acid. This acid eventually kills the bacteria that produced it and then a second type of bacteria begins growing to produce additional acids. Again, these acids eventually kill the second bacteria population. Finally, a third species grows and produces certain flavoring compounds that are characteristic of sauerkraut. These bacteria are always there; they start growing when the cabbage is mixed with salt. Yogurt, cheese, sausages, wines and beers, and soy sauce are all formed by the fermentation process. Many antibiotics are formed by fermentation. Specific bacteria or molds are grown which produce chemicals that are extracted and used for medicinal purposes. It is important to note that bacteria, yeast and molds have very useful functions and are not totally undesirable organisms.

Food Poisoning

Food poisoning, generally called *ptomaine poisoning*, occurs in many different ways. One type of food poisoning is produced by a bacteria called *Staphylococcus*. When *Staphylococcus* grows it forms a chemical which causes sickness. This type of food poisoning is usually associated with cream pastries and salads such as chicken salad. Symptoms of *Staphylococcus* poisoning include diarrhea and vomiting. This will be discussed in greater detail in Chapter 18.

Salmonella, another bacteria, also causes food poisoning. Here the ingestion of the organism itself brings on sickness. Symptoms resulting from the ingestion of the salmonella organism are usually similar but much more severe than those from *Staphylococcus* poisoning. Though food poisoning from both these organisms is unpleasant to endure, it usually does not prove fatal.

Botulism is a severe form of food poisoning produced by the organism known as *Clostridium botulinum*. This form of food poisoning can be fatal. The organism produces a chemical which is one of the most toxic substances known to man: 1 microgram (1 millionth of a gram) is enough to kill a million people. Botulism is most likely to occur in improperly processed, canned foods.

Clostridium perfringens is a food-poisoning organism that has become important in the last few years. One source of this food poisoning has been traced to holding roast beef under hot lights in restaurants. The warm condition stimulates the organism to grow to large numbers which, when eaten, cause a mild intestinal upset. It is possible that much of what is called the 24-hr flu is caused by this bacteria.

Preventing the Growth of Microbes

The primary basis of food processing is the prevention of
undesirable microbial growth. This can be done by killing the
microbes, reducing their number, or treating the food in such
a way that they do not grow. There are many ways to accomplish this. The heating of foods generally destroys many harmful organisms. Sterilization is a common form of heating. This
is the principle that canning, both home and industrial, is
based upon. Pasteurization is another form of heating which
involves the use of less heat than sterilization to reduce the
numbers of organisms. This reduction lengthens the shelf-
life of the food product. Radiation, another pasteurization
technique, though illegal in the United States, is used in Canada,
Israel, and The Netherlands in low doses to treat the surfaces
of mushrooms, potatoes, and strawberries. This reduces the
mold on these foods and increases shelf-life.

Filtration is a method of processing used to remove yeasts.
It is employed in the production of some vinegars, wines, and
beers. Filtering is especially desirable for use in these products since it does not destroy or change flavors as does heating
the food.

Environmental factors which do not destroy organisms but
prevent their growth are also important in food processing.
One of these controlling factors is temperature. Refrigeration
and freezing of foods lowers the environmental temperatures
to levels which do not allow the growth of many destructive
organisms. Holding foods at very high temperatures also prevents the growth of many organisms. A problem with holding
foods at high temperatures, i.e., using a steam table, is that
the high temperature causes destruction of many important
nutrients.

Controlling oxygen levels is also an environmental factor
which can prevent the growth of molds. An example of this
factor is found in the home production of jams and jellies.
The application of a layer of paraffin wax to the top of the jam
prevents oxygen from entering the jar and aiding the subsequent growth of molds. On a commercial basis, a vacuum
pump is utilized to remove the oxygen from the jar. However,
in some foods certain bacteria can grow in the absence of

oxygen. We will evaluate this problem later in the book with respect to canning procedures.

Chemicals can also be used as environmental factors. They can function as control measures which prevent microbes from growing. Changing the pH or acidity of a food by the addition of vinegar can inhibit the growth of many organisms. This is the method used to prevent growth in certain salad dressings.

Sugar and salt are also added to many sausages, hams, and bacon to increase their shelf-life. Many organisms require water to grow, and sugar and salt bind the water in such a way as to greatly reduce the availability of water to the microbes. This inhibits their growth and retards spoilage. These binding factors are known as humectants. The new hamburger-type dog food products are stable toward microbial deterioration at room temperature. In these products, meat and cereal are combined with enough salt and sugar to bind the water. This prevents the growth of the deleterious organisms. History reveals the use of this principle by the American Indians. During their travels and during the long winters they ate pemmican, made by mixing berries, a source of sugar and acid, with buffalo meat and nuts. The binding action effected by the sugar and the acid of the berries produced a very stable product. The American Indians invented the basis of the dog-food industry that has come into existence since the late 1960's.

Smoking foods is another old process that prevents the growth and decay of harmful organisms. Smoke from wood or charcoal coats the food with many chemicals that are highly toxic to the bacteria on the food. Smoking has been proved to also produce chemicals which are carcinogenic. This means that eating smoked foods could cause cancer in humans. Charcoal-grilled foods are very desirable to most of us because we like the taste, but it must be realized that carcinogenic materials are also ingested. This brings up the risk/benefit ratio which must be realized. The individual consumer must decide whether or not he should eat foods which could cause cancer, that is, should he take the risk in light of the high degree of acceptability of the food. The carcinogenic effects of such foods is still under investigation, but the consumer must be aware of the chemical content of the foods he eats so that he can make his decision.

Metabolic inhibitors—chemicals that when added to foods

prevent the metabolic processes of microbes—constitute another environmental factor for controlling deleterious organisms. Antibiotics function on this principle. In the production of some beers, certain metabolic inhibitors can be used instead of filtration or pasteurization, both of which destroy flavor. Thus a shelf-stable draft beer can be produced. Many people believe that such inhibitors should be included on the labels of food products. Their possible injurious effects will be discussed in a later chapter.

The control of water in food is also an important environmental factor used in preservation. The freezing of foods transforms liquid water into a solid form. In the solid form, ice, microbes cannot grow. Two benefits of freezing are (1) lowering the temperature of foods to slow the rate of chemical reaction, and (2) freezing of water into ice to make it unavailable to organisms and reactions.

Drying is another environmental factor similar to freezing in principle. Whereas freezing makes water unavailable for the growth of microbes by converting the liquid water into a solid state, drying renders water unavailable to microbes by removing it from the food. Smoking of foods is a form of surface drying which increases shelf-life. The use of humectants, which bind the water to make it unavailable, is another form of controlling the growth of microbes as mentioned above for sugar and salt.

Packaging is also an important environmental factor which combines many conditions to achieve the desired results in protecting foods. An example of the use of the effects of packaging may be found with the harvesting of unripe bananas. Unripe bananas emit a hormone vapor that aids in the ripening process and the subsequent packaging of unripe bananas in polyethylene bags traps this gas. Therefore environmental conditions are controlled to the extent that the bananas will achieve the desired degree of ripeness by the time they are ready for sale. The package also prevents infestation of insects and undesirable microbes. Overall, the first basis of food preservation is the control of undesirable microbes. Secondly, the process helps to slow down the chemical deteriorative reactions which also make a food eventually unacceptable.

CHAPTER 13

Heat Preservation—Canning

History of Heat Processing

As stated earlier, Napoleon was largely responsible for stim-
ulating the discovery of canning. Around 1740 Napolean needed
a means to supply meats, fruits, and milk to his troops during
lengthy stays away from home. He offered a prize to the person who discovered how to do this most effectively. In 1795 a
Frenchmen, Appert, invented the canning process which he
referred to as *appertizing*. His process involved placing food
in glass jars. After boiling the jars for a while he sealed
them shut with a cork which was wired down and covered
with wax. They were then cooked for an additional length of
time and afterwards held for about two months on the shelf.
During this time if some jars exploded he realized that the
food was not adequately processed so he would experiment
with longer boiling times. Although Appert did not understand
the principles behind his method, it won the prize and quickly
caught on as a method of preserving food.

At that time it was believed that the basis of the canning
process was that when the food was heated, the oxygen was
either forced out of the jar or reacted with the food in a manner which prevented the food from spoiling. Gay-Lussac, a
French chemist, strongly supported this idea, since he had a
method for testing for the presence of oxygen. He found that
food that was appertized did not contain oxygen. Canned foods
became popular in many parts of the United States and Europe
with the advent of this preservation process.

During the years 1820–1880 the owners of canning factories
played the roles of magicians. They would enter their plants
toward the end of the canning process wearing magician's
costumes and would mumble mystical incantations over the
vats and sometimes throw handfuls of mysterious white powder
into each vat. By adding the special powders they found they
could reduce the process time of these foods from 4 hr to 2 hr
in some instances. Many guilds developed which utilized these
techniques. Unknown to them the addition of these salts—so-

dium chloride or potassium chloride—raised the boiling point
of the water in which the foods were being cooked. Instead of
boiling at the normal boiling point of water, 212°F, the canned
foods were being processed at temperatures up to 240°F, thereby causing a reduction in total processing time. The reasons
for this will be explained later.

In 1870 some engineers discovered that the principle behind
the effects of the magical salts was their ability to raise the
temperature at which the foods were processed. They then
built retorts—large pressure cookers—to accomplish the same
purpose. Interestingly, the commercial retorts of this period
usually exploded after 6 or 7 months of use due to the lack of
adequate technology and high-quality steel for operating under
high temperatures. This inhibited the canning industry but
stimulated the iron industry to search for methods to produce
strong steel.

At that time many people believed that food spoiled as a result of spontaneous generation, the creation of living organisms
from non-living matter if oxygen were present—a theory that
was well supported by many religious groups. Finally in
1870, Pasteur discovered that microbes are present in all
foods and that in order to preserve foods the environmental
conditions of the foods had to be controlled to prevent microbial growth. He convinced people that the canning of
food was not based on the removal of oxygen, but that heat
killed the bacteria, yeasts, or molds in the food. It was
not until 1910 that the mathematics for the determination
of heat-processing times were discovered based on microbial death.

In 1930 Ball published the equations (based on the work of
Underwood and Prescott) which are the basis for the modern
canning industry. Even today many processors do not understand these formulas, and instead of using them still operate
on the trial-and-error basis used by Appert to find process
times required for new foods. In most cases this leads to overprocessing of the food. If a mathematical determination were
made to give the minimum safe cook time needed, better-quality
food would be produced, since overprocessing results in excessive nutrient destruction. There are no laws except in
California to govern the length of time for processing foods.

In 1973 a regulation was passed that all processors now have to register with the FDA and justify the safety of each process used.

Safety of Canned Foods

The safety of canned foods must be determined before the food products are released on the market. The determination of safety is made by a study of the organisms that would be most likely to pose the biggest problem in a given product. Microbiologists realize that the canning process removes the oxygen from the canned food product and, therefore, those organisms that grow in the absence of oxygen must be studied. For example, *Clostridium botulinum* grows in the absence of air and its spores are more resistant to heat treatment than most other organisms. Therefore, tests of canned foods for the presence of *Clostridium botulinum* showing that this organism is not present indicate that the less hardy organisms have also been destroyed. Because of this, all heat processes are based on destroying spores of *Cl. botulinum*, since it produces one of the most toxic chemicals known to man when it grows. The disease the toxin produces is called botulism. An amount the size of a penny is enough to kill everyone in the United States. About 20% of the people who contact botulism die.

A drop of liquid can be packed with 1 billion tiny microorganisms of various types. The same amount of food as in a drop can contain between 100 and 1 million of these organisms prior to processing. These various organisms are destroyed at different rates depending on the temperature used, as illustrated in Fig. 13.1.

An equation for predicting how many organisms would die in the canning process can be formulated based on this kind of data if the temperature profile during processing is known. In order for the organisms to be destroyed, heat must penetrate through the can into the interior of the contents. The slowest heating point in the can must be found and the processing variables of time and temperature adjusted in accordance with the factors necessary to kill the maximum number of organisms possible at this point. If the organisms are destroyed

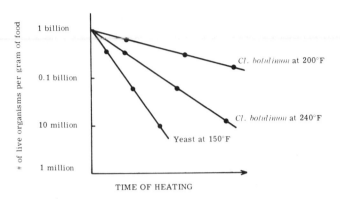

FIG. 13.1. EFFECT OF HEAT ON DEATH OF MICROORGANISMS

at the slowest heating point, it may be assumed that the organisms are destroyed at all other places within the can. In the
case of solid pack foods, such as ham or hash, the center of the
can is the slowest heating point. Therefore, the temperature
at that point versus time is used to determine the amount of
kill. In order to ensure safety of canned foods, all processors
have arbitrarily assumed that the most resistant and dangerous
organism, *Cl. botulinum*, is present at a level of greater than
1 billion per gm. Of course, this would generally not be true;
however, it does give an extremely high safety factor.

Calculations of the death of *Cl. botulinum* yield the following
safety factor: if there are only 100 organisms present at the
slowest heating point, the food would end up being processed
so that there is only 1 chance in 10 billion that the organisms
could survive, grow and produce toxin. All food processes for
canning theoretically operate within this safety factor. Hypo-
thetically, if a canning plant were large enough to manufacture
10 billion cans of a food product at one time, then one of the
cans should spoil. However, there are no canning plants in
operation that have the facilities to process this number of
cans in a single batch. The reason some commercial cans
spoil is due to: (a) processes based on trial and error that are
inadequate; (b) improper sealing of cans and subsequent re-
contamination; and (c) growth of heat-resistant microbes.

Commercial Canning over the Last 40 Years

In the last 40 years of commercial practices, approximately
800 billion cans of food products have been produced (up to

TABLE 13.1
DEATHS IN CANNED FOOD DUE TO BOTULISM

Year	Number of Deaths (Home Canned)	Number of Deaths (Commercial)	Commercial (Implicated Food)
1941	0	1	Mushrooms
1963	0	2	Tuna fish
1970	5	0	
1971	8	1	Vischyssoise
1972	4	0	
1973	1	1	Bell peppers
1974	6	1	Beef stew
1975	?	0	−
1976	?	0	−

December 31, 1972). Six incidents of contamination of *Cl. botulinum* in canned food were reported during 1973, but only one was due to commercially processed food. Unfortunately, more incidents have been reported recently due to under-processing of mushrooms, but no deaths have occurred. In the past 40 years there have been only 6 deaths from commer-cially canned foods, as shown in Table 13.1. In fact from 1925 to 1941 no deaths were reported from commercially canned foods. The reason that 6 deaths have occurred was that the retort (canner) operators failed to make certain the cans were processed at the specified temperature, or the can was not sealed properly and became recontaminated with the bacteria. Fortunately, *Clostridium botulinum* usually produces off-odors and gas, so a swollen can or off-odors once the can is opened are good indications that the food is contaminated and danger-ous. Death can still be avoided by cooking the canned food product at home prior to serving, since the toxin is not resis-tant to heat. As seen in Table 13.1, the foods that caused death were foods that can be eaten without heating.

Home Canning

Home-canned food has been responsible for about 3/4 of the outbreaks of botulism in the country over the past 70 years. In the last 20 years, home canning has resulted in almost 5 deaths per year because of improper canning procedures. In 1970 there were 6 reported outbreaks of botulism poisoning affecting 13 people, 5 of whom died. All were from home-canned food. In 1971 there were 9 outbreaks of food poisoning due to the consumption of home.-canned foods affecting 23 people. As seen in Table 13.1, 8 deaths occurred. In 1972 there were 24 cases of food poisoning from botulism resulting in 4 deaths, again from home-canned foods.

The failure of the home canner to check the operation of the pressure gauge on the pressure cooker is the chief error resulting in the spoiling of home-canned foods. Also, the sampling of home-canned foods prior to heating is a cause of deaths from food poisoning. In 1972 a woman opened a jar of home-canned green beans, tasted the beans, heated them and served them to her family. The family lived; she died. This shows how sensitive the toxin is to heat.

Nutrient Destruction in Canned Foods

The destruction of nutrients is the primary drawback of the canning process. The processing procedure used for destroying the dangerous organism *Cl. botulinum* results in the destruction of vital nutrients. The canning process itself destroys up to 30% of vitamin C. Preparation for canning fruits and vegetables requires washing, sorting, and blanching (scalding the vegetables or fruits in hot water or steam). Blanching the food is a mild heat treatment that destroys the enzymes in the fruits or vegetables that cause the production of off-odors, off-flavors, and off-colors during storage. The use of hot water or steam for blanching can cause a loss of up to 25% of the vitamin C. If the vegetables are reheated at home in preparation for serving, the possibility exists for the destruction of an additional 25% of the vitamin C. This results in a total loss of vitamin C that can be as high as 75%.

Other vitamins that are affected by heat treatment are thiamine and vitamin A. In a product such as a canned soup containing meat, approximately 10 to 20% of the thiamine is lost. Vitamin A losses equal 15 to 20% for the same type of product. These losses could be reduced if the manufacturer would combine the mathematics of nutrient destruction with the death of the organisms to optimize the process.

Nutritional labeling of certain foods as required by the Food and Drug Administration is creating an impetus to investigate the effect of heat-processing on nutrients in all kinds of foods. In the past, the food industry has been selling foods on the basis of flavor and texture acceptability, and thus far these criteria have been the most important considerations to the consumer. A recent survey of 50,000 homemakers all over the United States revealed that only 20% of those surveyed placed nutrition as the principal criterion for the selection of foods. However, this is changing slowly as the consumer becomes more aware of nutrition and the effects of additives on foods. Presently, there is a trend toward consumer advocation of government measures to control certain foods and certain food additives. This increased nutritional and food awareness is causing changes in the food industry (including the canning industry) to increase the value of processed foods. Also, data are being collected on the shelf-life of canned foods. It is known that they have a very long life since there is no oxygen in the can. How long, however, is not known. The various chemical reactions and nutrient loss rates are the main areas of research.

Improving the Quality of Heat-processed Foods

It is possible to process foods by methods that are not as nutritionally destructive as the normal retort canning procedure. For example, peas are normally processed in cans at 240°F for 35 min, destroying approximately 25% of the vitamin C. In the process of aseptic canning, peas are pumped rapidly through a tube heated on the outside by hot air or steam. They are heated for only 2 minutes at 350°F, which destroys less than 5% of the vitamin C, but the same amount of bacteria as in a retort pressure cooker. This is because at the higher temperature there is a much higher rate of bacteria kill as compared to nutritional losses. The sterile peas are then filled directly into sterile cans or stainless steel pouches. Peas processed this way have the taste and texture of fresh peas.

Other methods used to improve nutritional quality include agitating the cans, processing directly in foil pouches, and using direct gas flames for heating. Agitating the cans in the retort increases the rate of heating because the food inside the can rotates rapidly, distributing the heat evenly. Thus the

slowest heating point is no longer in the center but is distributed throughout the can. Foil pouches heat faster because they
are much thinner than a can for the same amount of food and
have a larger surface area for contact with the heating steam.
The use of a gas flame causes an even faster heating rate.
With steam, because of the danger and cost of creating high
pressure and temperature, the maximum temperature that can
be used is 250°F. Gas flames can heat at 2000°F and if the can
is rotated rapidly in the flame, the contents heat quickly without burning. Several food companies are now using these processes.

High-temperature Bacteria

Canned foods are not completely sterile. They are considered
to be commercially sterile. Bacteria that are more heat-
resistant than *Clostridium botulinum* remain in the cans but do
not grow at normal room temperature or produce any toxin.
These bacteria are known as thermophiles, and grow only at
high temperatures. For instance, if a shipment of canned foods
traveled by truck across the desert and was allowed to become
very hot (about 120 to 130°F) it would be possible for these
organisms to start to grow within the cans. This could turn
the food product sour and/or cause the formation of gas, subsequently causing the cans to explode. It is highly unlikely that
canned foods subjected to such conditions would ever reach
supermarket shelves, but in some cases they do. The consumer
should not use the cans, but call the local Food and Drug Administration so they can check the contents.

Aseptic Canning Line

CHAPTER 14

Cold Preservation—Refrigeration and Freezing

Principle of Refrigeration and Freezing

The lowering of temperature to slow down the growth of microorganisms and the chemical and biochemical reactions within foods is the principle behind the use of refrigeration and freezing for the preservation of foods. Almost 55% of the foods consumed at the present time are refrigerated or frozen. Another 30% of foods consumed are preserved by canning and 5% are dehydrated.

History of Cold Preservation

There are references to Roman emperors sending runners up into the mountains to bring down snow for cooling some of their foods and drinks. Refrigeration in the United States before the 1800's was accomplished by using ice cut from lakes and placing the chunks in an ice box. Ice was stored in huge ice houses for use in the summertime. The big drive for mechanical refrigeration began in the 1850's by the beer brewers who could not make lager beer in the summer. In 1860 mechanical refrigeration that utilized ammonia compressors was discovered to solve the needs of the brewers.

Meat packing was also responsible for increasing the demand for mechanical refrigeration. Prior to 1880 it was necessary for animals to be shipped live to the cities and then distributed to slaughterhouses. It was very expensive to ship the entire live animal and the meat plants wanted to be able to butcher their beef and then to ship it. The railroads were against this because this meant less profits, so the meat plants built their own railroad cars with refrigeration in which to ship the butchered beef. Eventually, they gained a monopoly on refrigerated cars by controlling the shipping of all meats and fresh produce until 1916 when an antitrust suit broke them up.

Mechanical home refrigeration was not standard until the 1920's but really did not become widespread until the early

1940's. Since that time no one would consider having a home
without a refrigerator.

Uses of Refrigeration

Foods have varying optimum temperatures at which they
should be refrigerated. Meats should be stored as cold as possible. Green bananas should not be refrigerated as the cold will
cause impairment of the ripening mechanism. Green tomatoes
will also fail to ripen if refrigerated. Potatoes, if chilled at too
low a temperature, have an enzyme system which will turn the
starches to sugars under this condition. It is well known, for
example, that unrefrigerated corn quickly loses its sweetness;
however, it is not common knowledge that tomatoes can lose
up to 40% of their vitamin C within 3 days after picking if held
at room temperature.

The average temperature for the prevention of senescence
(aging) for most fruits and vegetables is 35 to 40°F. Most
refrigerators operate at around 45°F, which is too high. When
senescence becomes evident the produce becomes soft, vitamin
C is depleted, and the resistance to microbes is lowered, with
the eventual growth of molds on the surface causing decay.

Increasing the length of storage in the refrigerator may be
accomplished by placing the food in a plastic bag. The film
inhibits loss of water, thereby preventing wilting. The film
must be slightly permeable to oxygen if fruits or vegetables
are being packaged. During storage conditions fruits and vegetables are burning sugars, and in order to do so they need
oxygen. Usually, the higher the oxygen levels, the faster the
burning of the sugars and the sooner senescence occurs. Therefore, packaging to keep oxygen levels low will help preserve
the food for a longer time. However, a destruction of tissues,
yielding acids and alcohol, will result if the oxygen level in the
package gets too low. For each fresh product the packaging
must be designed to balance the amount of water going out and
the amount of oxygen going in. This is the reason plastic potato
sacks have holes in them. The waxing of fruits is an old process that also helps preserve fresh produce in much the same
way as film packaging.

Ethylene is a gas used on fresh fruits and vegetables to induce ripening. For instance, oranges picked in Florida are

usually at various stages of ripening, and for marketing purposes it is desirable for all of them to be at the same stage.
For this reason the oranges may be placed in chambers and
exposed to ethylene. Ethylene, although a gas, is produced by
the plant itself as a growth-stimulating hormone. By spraying
it over the fruit, or using the film packaging to trap ethylene
within the bag, the ripening process is accelerated. The use
of film packaging can eliminate the need for prior spraying
with ethylene.

Holding Fresh Fruits and Vegetables

Though it is reasonable to assume that fresh produce when
refrigerated at home is stored under desirable conditions, it
is not reasonable to assume that it is as carefully handled
from the time it is picked to the time it reaches the supermarket. In fact, in part the opposite is true, especially with
fresh produce from local markets and supermarkets. Though
most supermarkets have produce stored in cold cases or over
ice, many do not refrigerate them and a great amount of nutritional deterioration takes place. It is hoped that future legislation with regard to the holding of food commercially will aid
in the upgrading of the nutritional quality of our food.

Freezing serves much the same purpose as refrigeration.
Both processes use low temperatures in order to slow the rate
of decay in foods. Freezing is more effective because the temperatures are much lower than refrigeration. Freezing also
converts liquid water into a solid, binding the water needed by
the microbes for growth.

Although frozen foods keep much longer than refrigerated
foods, they are not infinitely stable. Not all the water freezes
out when the food is frozen. At $-20°F$ as much as 10% of the
water can remain unfrozen in the food. Chemical reactions can
still go on in the unfrozen water, destroying food quality. Frozen foods actually have a relatively short shelf-life in comparison to canned foods because they are exposed to oxygen.

What Happens to Foods When They Are Frozen?

Physical Changes.—Textural damage takes place in foods
when they are frozen. Meats such as pork or fatty fish like
salmon toughen during frozen storage. Fruits and vegetables

become mushy when frozen, losing their natural crispness.

In addition to textural damage, a condition known as drip occurs. Thawed meat often exhibits a runny, red liquid that looks like blood. This liquid is not blood, but tissue water that the tissues can no longer hold. Freezing causes damage to the tissues to the extent that, once frozen and thawed, the food can no longer hold the original amount of water that was within the cells. This also makes the food seem dryer and tougher when eaten.

Package ice is another physical damage caused by freezing. For example, a frozen pizza may show ice crystals within the package. This is due to the evaporation of water from the food into the air space left in the package. This ice loss is not damaging for most foods, but it can be detrimental to frozen turkeys or chickens because the area from which the water evaporated can darken and become tough. This is called *freezer burn*. Elimination of the air space is the best way to prevent such ice build up. This is done by using a shrink wrap (very tight seal) or vacuum packaging to pull the film very close to the food surface. Unfortunately, in some foods like a pizza this is difficult to do.

Chemical Changes. — Chemical reactions which cause deterioration also occur in frozen foods. Rancidity is one of the most rapid chemical deterioration reactions in frozen foods. Foods such as fish and cured meats like ham, which contain unsaturated fats, are especially susceptible. The fats break down in oxygen and a rancid flavor develops very rapidly. However, the lower the temperature, the slower the rate of reaction so that at least several months of shelf-life are possible. Vacuum packaging helps to slow this down even further.

Browning, another chemical reaction, is especially evident in frozen fruits. Peaches tend to brown in frozen storage due to the presence of enzymes within the fruit. These enzymes cause some of the sugars in the fruit to react with oxygen and produce a brown color. The brown color is disagreeable only from an aesthetic standpoint. Browning in fruits can be prevented by packing the fruits in a heavily sugared syrup prior to freezing. This serves as a barrier to oxygen. They can also be blanched to destroy the enzymes, but this softens the fruit and causes a cooked flavor which is undesirable. Sulfur dioxide

TABLE 14.1
LENGTH OF STORAGE OF FROZEN FOODS

	Home Refrigerator Freezer 10°F (Months)	Home Frozen Food Locker 0°F (Months)	Industrial Food Locker −30°F (Months)
Beef	3	12	24
Chicken	2	6	13
Fish (fatty)	½	1	5
Corn	4	10	30
Bacon	1	3	7
Bread[1]	6	24	36

[1]Bread will toughen at a faster rate when refrigerated than if stored at room temperature.

is also used to slow this reaction, but it causes an off-flavor in many fruits.

Vitamin loss (usually vitamin C) is evident in frozen foods. The rate of loss is faster in frozen foods than in canned foods, though nutritional loss is much less than in fresh produce. For example, fresh strawberries lose 50% of their vitamin C in two weeks at 70°F but only 20% in one year at 0°F. Most vitamins are quite stable in frozen foods, and their quality remains quite high for a long time. Table 14.1 shows how long foods can be kept frozen.

Because of the high nutritional quality of frozen foods, the frozen-food industry has been growing rapidly, particularly the vegetable lines. The freezing process makes it possible to obtain good-quality vegetables all year round. Many people believe that frozen foods are of much higher quality than canned or fresh foods.

Thawing Frozen Foods

The highest-quality frozen food is produced by the fastest freezing method. Liquid nitrogen (−280°F) is currently the best method for freezing fruits and vegetables on a commercial basis. These foods are frozen in a matter of minutes in liquid nitrogen, whereas a home freezer requires more than 6 hr to freeze a similar amount of food.

The process of thawing operates on the same principle as freezing, i.e., faster thawing gives better quality. In fact very slow thawing may cause severe quality loss. Due to the inherent properties of ice and water, the thawing process takes 3 to 5 times longer than the freezing of food. Much of the nutritional damage that occurs may take place during the thawing process. The food industry has been looking at several different ways to thaw frozen foods to maintain high quality. An example is the suggestion to roast directly from the frozen state, as can be done presently with turkeys and chickens. Another is the frozen boil-in-the-bag vegetable pouches, which ensure rapid thawing without burning in the pot. Many foods can also be thawed and cooked in microwave ovens, which are being used extensively in hospitals and restaurants. Thawing at room temperature is the least recommended thawing method due to the probability of the growth of microorganisms while the food is on the counter top. This can lead to food poisoning.

One of the biggest problems is the handling of frozen foods after they leave the frozen food plant. Sometimes the truck that carries them breaks down and they thaw out, or they are left on the loading dock of the supermarket too long. In many cases stock clerks at supermarkets do not quickly fill the frozen food display, leaving the frozen food on a cart till it thaws. All these factors combine to cause physical and chemical changes that decrease quality and nutritional value. Thaw indicators placed on the frozen food package have been developed that would reveal to the consumer if a frozen-food product had been subjected to improper storing or handling conditions. The use of thaw indicators raises the problem of who pays for the loss. Many consumers wrongfully blame the manufacturers for spoiled food when it is really the error of the handler. Legislation may be needed in this area.

Questions About Freezing

(1) *How do frozen foods compare with canned and dehydrated foods from a nutritional standpoint?*

Due to processing procedures, frozen foods are the most nutritious and are very desirable from an acceptability standpoint in most cases.

(2) *Can foods be refrozen?*

The refreezing of foods is not forbidden, as is sometimes believed, providing that the conditions under which the foods were thawed and held did not allow the growth of poisonous microorganisms. Unfortunately, since most people have little knowledge of the microbial problems that can develop, they should not refreeze food.

Boil-In-Bay Type Package

CHAPTER 15

Dehydrated Foods

Currently, a wide variety of dehydrated food products are available for home use. Dry milk, instant coffee (coffee machines use dehydrated coffee), hamburger mix products, and many pharmaceuticals are produced by the dehydration process. This chapter will discuss the aspects of how dehydrated foods are made.

There is very little recorded history with regard to dehydrated foods, though sun-drying and smoking were probably the first methods of drying foods to be used. A product that is commonly sun-dried at the present time is raisins. The major developments in drying took place in war time when shelf-stable foods were needed for the military.

Basis of the Dehydration of Foods

The method of food preservation by drying is based on the principle that microbial growth and chemical reactions can only occur when enough water is present. By removing the water down to a certain level the deteriorative reactions are prevented. The level necessary to preserve foods is established by the term water activity (A_w), or water availability. In fresh-tissue foods the water activity is equal to 1 and growth and deterioration can take place. Dry foods have a water activity much less than 1 $(A_w \approx 0.2)$ so that microbes cannot grow in them; however, certain chemical reactions can occur to reduce shelf-life. The special *soft-moist* burger-type dog foods on the market today have an $A_w \approx 0.8$. These are at the level of water availability where microbes cannot grow, but enough water is present so that the food could be eaten without rehydration. These foods are similar to fig newtons, cheese, and fruit cake. Rather than removing all the water, sugar or salt is added. The sugar or salt ties up the water, making it unavailable for microbes, thus preserving the food. This is one form of dehydration.

In the normal method used to dehydrate foods, it is necessary to heat them in some manner to drive off the water. Since

104

many nutrients are unstable to heat, destruction of nutrients can take place during dehydration. Loss of vitamin C, vitamin B_1, and vitamin A is common in the dehydration process, but the amount lost depends on the process used. Protein is not affected by the dehydration process, nor is it greatly affected by canning or freezing methods. The eating quality in terms of flavor, color, and odor can also be adversely affected by this process.

Methods of Drying

Sun drying, where fruits or vegetables are laid out on racks in the sun, usually takes about 3 or 4 days. It is still used today because it is cheap. For example, raisins are sun-dried grapes. Bacterial growth is a drawback in this drying process because the time required makes it possible for molds or bacteria to grow on the surface of these foods. Chemical reactions occurring during this drying process are important in the production of flavor and color, but would be undesirable during storage of most dried foods.

Sun drying is a process that is at the mercy of the weather, unlike other forms of food preservation. Insects are also a problem in sun drying. Chad, a country in Africa, has a large fish-drying industry; 10% of the dry weight of the finished product is fly larvae deposited on the fish during the drying process. This certainly would be unacceptable in the United States.

Sun-drying causes the largest loss of vitamins of any of the drying processes due to the length of time necessary to dry the food. For example, peaches lose 50% of their vitamin C. About 100 years ago people tried to discover how to dry without using the sun. Tray drying and tunnel drying were invented to accomplish this purpose. In tunnel drying, the sun is replaced with hot, dry air blowing at high velocity in the opposite direction over food passing through a chamber on a moving belt. The air supplies the heat to evaporate the water and the air also removes the water. Racks with trays containing food, either moving through the chamber or remaining stationary, accomplish the same effect; this is called tray drying.

The humidity of the air in the dryers must be low for dehydration to take place rapidly. The air velocity must also be

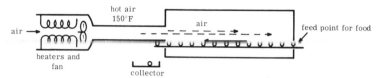

FIG. 15.1. TYPICAL TRAY DRYING PROCESS

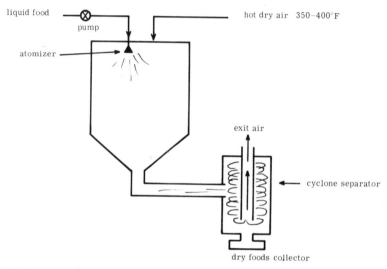

FIG. 15.2. TYPICAL SPRAY DRYING PROCESS

controlled so that the food is not blown off the tray or belt. A typical process is shown in Fig. 15.1.

Tray drying and tunnel drying can accomplish in 6 to 15 hr what takes several days for sun drying. The shorter drying time does not destroy as many nutrients as sun drying and gives a better quality food. Less than 10% of the vitamin C is lost using this process for fruits. Less than 20% of the vitamin A is destroyed in carrots. The big problem with tray-dried foods is that they shrink up and are hard to rehydrate. New processes are being developed to prevent this. Spray drying is a drying process utilizing a large chamber (60 to 100 ft tall, 20 ft in diameter). Foods such as milk and coffee are sprayed into the chamber along with very hot air at high velocity, as seen in Fig. 15.2. Drying can be accomplished in seconds be-cause of the high temperature and very fine spray. This results in a great reduction in nutrient loss as compared to tray, tun-

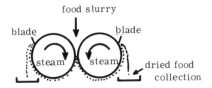

FIG. 15.3. TYPICAL DRUM DRYING PROCESS

nel, and sun drying. For example, only about 5% of vitamin C
is destroyed in a liquid food. Most dry milk, and instant tea
and coffee are made this way, as are desiccated liver and
yeast.

Another method of drying food slurries (mashed potatoes is
an example) is accomplished by drum drying. One method of
drum drying utilizes two rotating cylinders with a very small
space between them, as seen in Fig. 15.3. Steam is contained
within the cylinders and the slurry is dripped between the
cylinders. The slurry sticks to the cylinder surface, dries out,
and is scraped off the cylinder as it rotates. Drying is accomplished in a few minutes with greater nutrient loss than spray
drying but less than tray drying and sun drying. It is used for
slurried foods like mashed potatoes or tomato puree that are
too viscous to spray.

Freeze-drying is the best dehydration process available at
the present time. For example, in making freeze-dried coffee,
coffee is poured about 1/4-in. deep into trays. The trays are
placed in blast freezers (−40°F) and, when frozen, into a chamber connected to a vacuum pump. Heat is applied in this chamber to the frozen layers once the vacuum is pulled. The heat
supplies the energy to sublime (evaporate) the ice directly into
a vapor. The evaporated water travels into a second chamber
where it is refrozen on a condenser surface. The vacuum prevents the ice from melting and pulls out the residual air so that
the water vapor can move rapidly to the condenser surface.
The vacuum does not *suck* out the water, as is commonly de-
picted in advertisements. The advantage of keeping the food
frozen is that it does not shrink. This makes rehydration much
easier. The overall process is shown in Fig. 15.4.

Because the food is frozen and is at a low temperature during
drying, over 6 to 8 hr are needed to dry the food. In spite of
the long time necessary, little nutrient destruction occurs. For

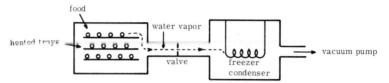

FIG. 15.4. TYPICAL FREEZE-DRYING PROCESS

example, less than 1% of vitamin C is destroyed in fruits and less than 5% of thiamine in dried pork because of the low temperature. The process is not used much, however, because it is prohibitively expensive. It costs much more to operate the 3 states of freeze-drying (freezing, running a condenser, and pulling a vacuum) than it does to tray-, tunnel- or spray-dry. Freeze-drying costs over 15 times more to remove a pound of water from a food than spray drying (some foods like nonfat dry milk have 19 lb of water for every pound of solids).

After dehydration, foods must be carefully packaged to prevent any further quality and nutritional losses. The package must act as a barrier to both oxygen and water. The types of chemical deterioration taking place during storage are discussed in the next chapter.

CHAPTER 16

Chemical Deterioration of Foods

A Review of Food Stabilities

Fresh foods deteriorate by 3 basic mechanisms: microbial growth, senescence, and wilting. Initially, fresh foods have the highest nutritional value but are subject to rapid decrease in nutritional quality after they are harvested as a result of natural aging. Refrigerator shelf-life is very short for most of them, so that fresh foods are relatively unstable. Sanitation, packaging and proper refrigeration extend the usable shelf-life.

Canned foods have a very long shelf-life, up to several years in some instances. Initially, however, the nutritional quality, particularly the vitamin content, of canned foods is not very high because of the high temperature used in processing. As much as 50% of vitamin C can be destroyed by canning. Canned foods cannot offer the textural quality of fresh foods either, because the heating process changes the texture. However, once a food is canned, very few changes in nutritional quality or texture take place because of the protection afforded by the can, unless they are held at high temperature.

Frozen foods have the highest overall nutritional quality if consumed within their shelf-life period. Some textural and nutrient destruction is evident but not to a high degree. The lower the temperature during storage, the longer the shelf-life and the less the destruction. Shrinkage or vacuum packaging is also necessary to prevent freezer burn.

Nutrient losses are a major problem in dry foods even though most of the water has been removed. Rancidity and browning are two chemical reactions that occur in dried foods to make them unacceptable after a period of time. It is important to package dry foods properly to prevent light from striking the foods and oxygen and moisture from getting into them. Light, oxygen, and moisture can initiate undesirable chemical reactions.

Nutrient Losses in Dry Foods

An example of loss of vitamin C is shown in the storage studies of powdered orange juice of less than 1% moisture content. It has been found that after 9 months, only 5% of the vitamin C disappears. Destruction increases as moisture content increases, so it is important to keep dried foods in moisture-free conditions. This same powdered juice would lose 50% of the vitamin C in 7 days if the moisture rose to 4% because of poor packaging or a hole developing in the package.

Temperature is also an important factor in the destruction of vitamins during storage, as is the case with dried pork. The higher the temperature of storage, the faster is the loss of nutritional quality. For example, the pork in a dried soup mix would lose 50% of thiamine in 70 days if held at 80°F and 50% loss in less than one month at 100°F. Thus low-temperature storage is needed for dry foods as well as good packaging.

Rancidity

Rancidity caused by oxidation of the unsaturated fats contained in foods is a major problem in dried foods. Rancidity in dried foods is prevalent because removal of water accelerates its development. The unsaturated fats react with oxygen and the trace metals present in foods act as catalysts to produce free radicals and peroxides, which can destroy many vitamins such as A, C, and E, decrease the nutritional value of protein, destroy pigments bleaching the food, produce toxins, and cause off-odors and off-flavors. Of course, some degree of rancidity is accepted in certain dry sausages and potato chips.

Preventing rancidity reactions in foods can be accomplished by several means. Since light catalyzes the reaction, an opaque package should be used. Removing oxygen by vacuum packaging is an important factor in the preservation of dried foods. Keeping temperatures low and controlling water content are also important. If the food is overdried, it will become rancid rapidly, so an optimum moisture content must be found.

The addition of antioxidants, which react with the free radicals and peroxides, slows down the development of rancidity in frozen and dried foods. Vitamin E is a natural antioxidant but is not used often in foods due to its high cost and the fact that it is not a very effective antioxidant. BHA and BHT are syn- thetic antioxidants that accomplish the same purpose; they need to be added only in very low levels since they are extremely effective. Ascorbic acid (vitamin C), EDTA and citric acid also prevent rancidity by tying up the trace metals so that they can- not activate the rancidity reaction. They are called chelating agents in labels on food packages since they bind the metals, making them unable to react with the unsaturated fats. Thus additives can be used to slow down the reaction and increase shelf-life.

Browning

Non-enzymatic browning is a reaction that occurs during storage of dried foods. This browning is a reaction of sugars and some amino acids causing the brown color, very much like that which develops in fresh-cut apples or in storage of frozen peaches. The latter are enzymatic reactions, however, and occur much faster. Toasting bread is a similar reaction but is desirable in that it produces a familiar flavor. The undesirable browning reaction that occurs between sugar and protein pro- duces a toughening of the food during storage. This makes the protein undigestible and thus reduces the nutritional value of the food.

Prevention of non-enzymatic browning can be accomplished by the removal of certain sugars such as glucose from dry foods. The reduction of water content also prevents the action of non-enzymatic browning. Again, good packaging increases shelf-life. The only chemicals that can prevent the browning reaction are the various sulfite salts; however, they can only be used in certain foods because of the off-flavor created and the fact that it destroys vitamin B_1. Normally, it is only used for some vegetables and fruits.

Packaging Uses

Packaging films accomplish a reduction in rancidity and non- enzymatic browning in dehydrated and frozen foods. Packaging prevents reactions which would occur in the presence of light and also protects the food from insects, microbes, and rodents.

It is also vital for aroma protection, either keeping good flavor
in or undesirable flavors out. Packaging also serves as a
means for shipping, advertising, and providing nutritional information for the product as well as helping to give information
about the shelf-life of a food.

Open Dating

Demands for open dating policies for the purpose of marking
foods with shelf-life expiration dates are increasing steadily.
At the present time all food packages in interstate commerce
and most intrastate-shipped foods have a code date stamped on
them indicating the place and the day the food was manufactured. Since there are approximately 10,000 different codes
utilized, it is very difficult for a consumer to know when the
product was packaged. Many consumer groups, therefore, have
decided that it is necessary to enact legislation to enforce the
open dating of foods. However, open dating can have several
definitions.

Kinds of Open Dating.—The *date of manufacture*, which involves the translation of existing codes into real dates, is one
form of open dating. This could be done very easily and would
be of benefit to the consumer. A *freshness date* is a date by
which the food should be consumed to obtain maximum quality
from the product. If the product is mishandled, the date could
prove to be meaningless. A *pull date* is a date after which the
product should not be consumed. Some companies are utilizing
pull dates at the present time, since they know the shelf-life
of the food under normal conditions in the package system they
are using.

Open dating of foods should encourage the shippers and supermarket personnel to rotate stock. Many times food companies
are blamed for producing stale foods when the undesirability
of the product was in reality caused by improper handling, i.e.,
restocking shelves from front to back instead of from back to
front.

Consumer rotating of stock to seek the freshest product
would not be a problem once the consumers were convinced
that stores were rotating stocks correctly to ensure the highest
quality. A store in Ohio that studied open dating on a government research project in 1972 found that initially consumers

would search for the dates of the freshest foods and pull them out. However, once convinced that the store was handling the products correctly, they ceased to do this. Overall, consumers benefited from higher quality products and higher nutritional value. There was a 50% reduction in returns of food to the supermarket, since less foods were spoiled.

Open dating on frozen foods could be utilized, but even more effective would be the use of a thaw indicator, as previously mentioned. This indicator could consist of test strips affixed to the package that would change colors if the package was thawed and/or refrozen. Such thaw indicators would also en-courage shippers, handlers, and retailers of frozen foods to be more careful with their handling practices, thereby benefiting the consumer.

CHAPTER 17

Chemical Preservation—Food Additives

History

As with other food preservation techniques, the use of chemicals to preserve food has a long history. Perhaps one of the oldest processes is the prehistoric practice of smoking and drying. Of course, at that time no one knew the basis of smoking as a chemical preservation process. Today it is realized that the food is preserved by the heat and the chemicals in the smoke deposited on the surface of the food, which help prevent the growth of deteriorative organisms. Fermentation is another ancient practice that was not well understood by its users. In this process, a desirable organism grows and produces substances such as acids or alcohol which inhibit the growth of undesirable microbes.

Salts and spices were used much later to preserve meats. Most of the early explorers carried with them on their expeditions a salted, partially dried meat that had the same consistency as jerky. Somewhere along the time chain it was discovered that combining the salt with acids produced by microbes could also be used to preserve food and give it a new flavor. This is the process of pickling.

Chemical preservation can be divided into two categories according to function: (1) the use of chemicals to control or prevent growth of microbes, and (2) the use of chemicals to control non-microbial deteriorative reactions such as rancidity. By the nature of some of these chemicals the foods also become flavored. Other additives are used to improve color, texture, flavor, odor, and the nutritional value of foods.

Fermentation Preservation

Fermentation is one of the best-known methods of food preservation. During fermentation, conditions are set up for the incomplete metabolism of the sugars in a food. Thus, instead of carbon dioxide and water being produced, many intermediates are formed, such as lactic acid and acetic acid. The latter is the principal acid in vinegar, the former the principal acid formed in fermented dairy products. If oxygen is limited one of the best-known fermentations takes place—the conversion of sugar to alcohol in wines and beers. These acids and alcoholes prevent the growth of undesirable organisms and thus make the food more stable. It is interesting in that, because metabolism is incomplete, the energy value of the food is not reduced to any great extent. Typical fermented foods are wine, beer, olives, cheese, and sauerkraut.

Chemical and Microbial Inhibitors

Many foods cannot be preserved by the fermentation method mentioned above. Chemical and microbial inhibitors must be added to these foods to impart stability. By far the most used microbial inhibitors for foods are table salt (sodium chloride) and sugar (sucrose). These inhibit microbial growth by binding the water, making it less available for biochemical reaction, as was discussed under "Dehydration" in Chapter 15. This is the method used in making jams, jellies, and cured hams. Other chemicals which do the same job are glycerol and propylene glycol which are added to the soft, moist, burger-type pet foods.

Acid is another good microbial inhibitor. This occurs naturally during fermentation. Industrially, citric acid, acetic acid, and phosphoric acid are added to lower the pH to a value where most pathogenic organisms cannot grow. Thus, mayonnaise has vinegar (acetic acid) added to it so that it does not have to be sterilized by heating under high temperature.

Some inhibitors have a direct effect on the metabolism of the microbes, thus preventing their growth. An example is benzoic acid which is found in high concentration in cranberries (about 4 to 5%). Others are calcium propionate which is added to bread, and sorbic acid which is added to beverages. Some spices are felt to have a similar effect.

Synthetic inhibitors such as the paraben compounds are introduced into fresh food wrappers to prevent surface growth of molds. Antibiotics, another form of growth inhibitors, have also been used in some procedures such as a dip for fresh fish. This was finally stopped, since many processors were relying on the dip rather than on good sanitation. Antibiotics are still used in animal feed, but the use is declining as better sanitation procedures are introduced.

A new method for extending the shelf-life of fresh meat is to give it a spray of dilute chlorine solution. This destroys some of the spoilage bacteria present on the surface. This method will become more popular in the future thereby benefiting the consumer by giving him a more stable product.

Flavoring Agents

Sugar and Salt.—Many food additives are used for purposes other than preventing the growth of organisms. Salt and sugar are frequently used to change flavor. Sugar consumption in the United States amounts to about 102 lb/person per year and consumption of salt is about 15 lb/person per year. Sugars such as glucose and corn syrup account for another 12 lb/yr. All other food additives including spices and proteins account for only another 10 lb/yr per person.

Artificial Sweeteners.—Artificial sweeteners have had an interesting and sobering history. Dulcin which was used in the early 1900's and cyclamates which were used up to 1963 were removed from the market because later research showed they might produce cancer. The only artificial sweetener consumed today is saccharin, and recent research shows that it also may be dangerous. Artificial sweeteners are important for diabetics and others on sugar-restricted diets, but the necessity for the average masses to consume large amounts of artificial sweeteners is nutritionally dubious. Advertising and snacking habits have greatly increased the consumption of foods with artificial sweeteners. Of course, if people cannot control their appetite, it may be better to drink diet pop than 10 cans of sugar-sweetened pop a day which could add 1000 to 1500 calories to the diet rather than only 20.

Alternative sources for sweetening agents are being investigated. There is a sweetening agent present in the rind of a grapefruit that is 2000 times sweeter than sugar, but it has not been tested for safety to date. Aspartame, a synthetic compound composed of two amino acids, is a sweetening agent that has not shown any toxic or carcinogenic properties in tests currently under way. It is believed that this sweetening agent will ultimately prove to be completely safe because of its ability to be digested in a manner similar to the other amino acids.

An interesting food from Africa called Miracle Fruit contains a sweetener that makes all foods consumed taste sweet for a period of 4 hr after eating. Similarly, a compound in artichokes has been found to have the same effect.

Organic Flavors.—There are over 50 chemical companies that produce flavor compounds for foods. Producing these flavors can be accomplished in one of two ways. An analysis of many of the components of a natural food flavor can be determined by trained chemists simply by tasting a flavor. Through their ability to recognize taste characteristics of the various constituents of a food they can make up a given flavor from a few individual chemical compounds. It is very difficult to get the exact flavor, since flavors can be made up of thousands of different compounds in quantities as minute as several parts per million. Some of these would be toxic if consumed in large amounts, but are harmless when present in traces. For example, acetone occurs in the natural extract of coffee flavor at less than 1 part per million and is necessary for the flavor. By itself acetone is the principal ingredient in nail polish remover and would cause severe liver damage if consumed.

Once the chemist isolates and identifies the various chemicals from the natural flavor he will begin mixing them from commercial supplies on hand to reproduce the natural flavor. The necessity for making artificial flavors is based on the fact that natural flavors are very expensive to produce in large quantities. For example, it takes five tons of bananas to produce one pint of banana oil, which gives a natural banana flavor. It is a lot easier to mix together synthetic ingredients to get the same flavor. One of the most famous of the flavoring agents is MSG (monosodium glutamate). It is a principal flavor in meat and adds meaty flavor and mouth feel to soups. We consume about $1\frac{1}{2}$ lb/person/yr. MSG is the sodium salt of a natural amino acid, but is usually produced by a microbial fermentation rather than extracting it from a food.

The other method of isolating flavor components is by the use of special electronic instruments. Usually a gas chromatograph is used first. This separates the odor or flavor of a food into the various components, which are then analyzed on more complicated instruments. These instruments can be used to identify all the components in a flavor. For example, an analysis of coffee shows that it is made up of over 400 different components. The scientist can then mix the various chemicals together to see which ones would produce the flavor closest to natural coffee. These instruments are used in production as well. Since the flavor of roasted coffee beans can vary from batch to batch as well as from variety to variety, a gas chromatograph is utilized to determine the combination of beans necessary to maintain a uniform flavor in the coffee product. This way you can always be sure that you are getting the same coffee flavor in your favorite brand.

Spices.—Spices are utilized basically to enhance the flavor of foods. The quest for spices, especially salt, was the major thrust behind many early explorations. Many spices have metabolic effects that aid in the preservation of foods by preventing microbial growth. This technique was utilized extensively at the time of the explorations. Spices are added in the home as well as in industry to aid in food acceptance.

Coloring Agents

There are two different types of food coloring agents: natural coloring agents, which are extracted from foods, and synthetic coloring agents, which are usually synthesized from coal tar or petroleum products. Carotene extracted from carrots is an example of a natural coloring agent. Violet #1 is an example of a colorant made from coal-tar. It was used for stamping the grades of meat on animal carcasses until it was shown in some tests to be carcinogenic to rats, and was then removed from use in foods. Many other coal-tar derivatives have proved to be carcinogenic and were removed from the market; there are also many that are not carcinogenic.

An example of the use of synthetic coloring agents can be seen in Florida oranges. When these oranges are picked at the state of ripeness, they are mottled green in color. They are sprayed to ensure a desirable orange color because of the competition with California oranges which are naturally orange in color when ripe. If people did not mind eating green oranges, the color would not have to be used.

Other compounds are used to stabilize or cause a color change in foods. One of the most important is sodium nitrite. When added to meat, it combines with the meat pigment to produce the

familiar pink color, found in frankfurters, ham, and other cured
sausage. Nitrite also adds some flavor and has some antimi-
crobial action. This is the reason sodium nitrite is used in the
production of canned cured meat products. It has been found
that nitrite either reduces the heat resistance of *Clostridium
botulinum* or inhibits growth, so less heat processing is needed.
This helps to preserve the texture and nutritional value of the
food.

Other compounds used to preserve color are the various
forms of sulfite. Sulfite compounds are applied to fruits and
vegetables to inhibit the browning reaction. Vitamin C has a
similar effect.

Functional Additives

Basically, the functional additives are those utilized to impart
chemical and physical stability to foods.

Emulsifiers and *surfactants* are chemicals with surface-active
properties which allow the structure of the food material to be
maintained. For example, in the manufacture of salad dressing
a surfactant would be added to prevent the separation of the two
phases that would naturally occur. Monoglycerides and diglycerides are common surfactants added to foods. Other functional additives are the Tweens and the Spans, which are synthetic chemicals that function as surfactants. They are nontoxic to the body because they are not digested. They are used
quite often since they are cheaper than natural emulsifying
agents. A natural type of surfactant is lecithin. It is extracted
from egg yolks and especially soy beans. Other uses of surfactants are in the manufacture of bread, where they help to
prevent staling during storage. Surfactants are used in juices
to prevent settling and in coffee cream to prevent separation.

Anti-caking agents are chemicals which when added to dry
foods such as salt or powdered sugar absorb water prefer-
entially so that the product does not stick together. This allows
the material to be free-flowing. Silicates are added to salts
to prevent caking and to yield an easy-pouring material. Corn-
starch is usually added to powdered sugar for the same reason
in the food industry when huge containers are involved. Otherwise the sugar would not flow.

Oxidizing agents are chemicals added to various kinds of

flours to render a better functioning protein. This means that bread will retain its structure after rising and baking, resulting in a desirable structure and texture in the finished loaf. Bromates and vitamin C are some of the chemicals which are utilized for this purpose.

The *binding* and *thickening agents* are protein, gums and starches, which when added to foods, help bind water giving a thick gravy or heavy syrupy texture. For example, the manufacture of cream-style corn requires the addition of a starch to produce the creamy texture. Since many natural starches and gums lose their ability to hold water after the foods are processed, some synthetic starches and gums are used that will hold up better during processing. Some starches are also added to salad dressing to increase the viscosity (fluid thickness) and thus decrease separation.

The chemicals BHA, BHT, and vitamin E are *antioxidants* which combine with the free radicals from oxidized fats in foods to prevent rancidity from developing. Although BHA and BHT have been shown to be somewhat toxic in rats, these compounds were being fed at high levels equaling up to 5% of the diet. In human foods BHA and BHT are consumed in very low levels equaling less than 100 parts per million. The use of baboons for testing BHA and BHT showed the compounds to be harmless. Since the chemical breakdown pathways of these animals are similar to man's, BHA and BHT are considered to be harmless for human consumption. This again points out the necessity of proper animal testing and the extrapolation of the data to humans.

The *metal chelating agents* are another type of antioxidant. Vitamin C, citric acid and EDTA are metal chelating agents which bind the trace metals present in food. These trace metals catalyze the lipid oxidation reaction. Use of chelating agents helps to preserve food for a longer period of time.

Vitamins, Minerals, Proteins, and Amino Acids

These ingredients are not functional in nature and their addition to foods is specifically to increase the nutritional value of the product. There are several bases for addition of nutrients to foods based on policies set by the National Academy of

Sciences. The three general bases for considering the addition of nutrients are:

(1) *Restoration*. The addition of nutrients to a food that were lost during processing to restore its original value. An example would be adding vitamin C to a sterilized fruit juice.

(2) *Enrichment*. The addition of nutrients to a food for which specific standards have been set. An example is bread which has certain standards for the B vitamins and iron which were established to supply a deficiency in the diets of most Americans.

(3) *Fortification*. The addition of one or more nutrients to foods for which there are no standards. Examples would be synthetic substitutes for fruit juices to which vitamin C is added since it would be in the normal food.

It should be mentioned that the policies set by the FDA help prevent over-addition of nutrients to prevent any dietary imbalance or cause any harm. A question still remains today as to whether snack foods should be fortified to supply vitamins, minerals and protein in relationship to calories. Many people feel that since we eat so many snacks we should fortify them. Others feel that this is unnecessary, since even the snack eaters get enough of the other nutrients from their regular foods.

Additives in Bread

A discussion of the additives found in bread will be used to summarize the kinds and functions of additives used in foods. Initially, when flour is milled it is yellow in color, produces bread of low loaf volume, and makes an unstable, inelastic dough. This flour must be oxidized in order to develop the protein so that a good-texture bread is obtained. This can be accomplished by allowing the dough to sit for several months or by the addition of additives to the flour to develop the protein. For example, the addition of ascorbate would oxidize the protein in the flour to develop it. Bromate and iodate would also serve to develop the protein. To whiten the flour, hydrogen peroxide, benzoyl peroxide, or lipoxidase is added to bleach the pigments to give a more desired whiteness. Milk solids are added to increase the nutritional quality of the bread; they are also important for increasing the elasticity of the dough. The sugar, lactose, found in milk solids is important for forming the crust

flavor. During the toasting of bread, the lactose reacts to produce the desired darkening and flavor. Besides being added
for its flavoring capabilities, salt is added to help control bacterial growth so that only the yeast can grow during fermentation. The salt also helps to toughen the dough so it is easier to
work with. Sugar is added not only for flavor but also as food
for the yeast during the fermentation process. Lysine may be
added to bread to increase its nutritional value, since gluten,
the protein present in bread, is a poor-quality protein. Functional additives include emulsifiers which tend to prevent
staling. Antioxidants are also added to lengthen the shelf-life
during storage. Calcium propionate, an acid, is added to bread
to control moldiness and softening which could be caused by
growth of undesirable bacteria. Vitamins and iron are also
added, since bread serves as a vehicle for transportation of
B vitamins and iron into the diet of many Americans. In this
case the addition of vitamins implies both partial restoration
and enrichment. As we have seen, many chemicals can be
added to white bread to increase its shelf-life and improve
its quality.

Summary

As will be pointed out in Chapter 20, additives are used only
when physiological safety has been proved at the levels consumed. All chemicals or foods can cause harm if overcon-
sumed. Proper use should not be a problem. The Food and
Drug Administration also requires that additives cannot be used
to disguise spoiled or poorly processed foods and that they
should be effective for their intended purpose.

CHAPTER 18

Food-Borne Diseases

The diseases discussed in this chapter are those that occur as the result of consumption of foods which carry toxic materials. As should be obvious by now, sanitation, proper processing, and preparation of foods should prevent diseases. However, since they still occur, we should understand something about their origin. It will also become evident that *ptomaine poisoning* is really a variety of illnesses caused by food.

Food Infection

Food infection is caused by the presence of bacteria within food that can grow very rapidly within the intestinal tract of humans, producing diarrhea, vomiting, and other unpleasant symptoms. *Salmonella, Shigella* and *Clostridium perfringens* are bacteria that can grow in foods as a result of improper handling. When consumed, these bacteria subsequently cause food poisoning. The reasons that they contaminate foods will be discussed below along with the methods of prevention.

Food Intoxications

Food intoxications are caused by organisms that grow on foods and produce harmful or lethal toxins. *Clostridium*, some molds and *Staphylococcus* species produce harmful toxins which can cause diarrhea and even death. These and their prevention will be discussed below. This is especially important since there are five times as many diseases reported from improper handling of foods in the home and food-service establishments as are caused by industry.

Mold Intoxication.—Poisoning from molds which produce toxins is uncommon in the United States but has occurred in other parts of the world. In the Orient, cooked rice that is allowed to sit at room temperature is susceptible to the formation of a very lethal mold. This black mold, *Aspergillus* *flavus*, produces a toxin that, if fed to ducks or turkeys in small doses, would kill them. It is suspected of causing death in many young children in the Orient. The toxin can also cause cancer from the consumption of low doses over a long period of time; thus foods containing the toxin are impounded and destroyed by the FDA.

Another potent toxin, *ergotamine*, is produced from the mold *Claviceps purpurea*. Many thousands of Russians died during World War II from consuming wheat which became contaminated because it was left in the field during the winter and not harvested until the following spring. One should never consume cereal products that have a purple mold growing on them, since it could be this organism.

Obviously, the answer with respect to prevention of disease from mold is to either handle grains and cereals properly or to find methods to detect the toxin and destroy the contaminated food.

Parasite Infections.—Amoebic dysentery is caused by a parasite common to the Orient. At the present time it is very difficult to kill this parasite once it is in the body, so it is possible for humans to carry it around for many years. Schistosomiasis, another infection, is one of the most prevalent diseases in the world, though it is not common in the United States. This is caused by a parasite transmitted by snails and afflicts people who work in rice paddies. The snails infect the humans, allowing the parasite to enter the body. The afflicted person will waste away since the parasite feeds on the blood and causes anemia. Life expectancy after infection is about 2 years. There is a medicine that can combat this disease but it has been proved to have mutagenic effects in rats, that is, it causes mutation. The question of the advisability of the use of the medicine is under dispute since it probably will also cause human mutations; however, no other drug has been found effective.

Trichinella is a parasite carried in pork. It can cause liver and brain damage and eventually death if the pork is eaten. There has been little evidence of this parasite in USDA-inspected meat over the last 40 years, but the disease is still evident in areas where people consume meat that had not been inspected. This is because unsanitary pens are used to keep the pigs. Thorough cooking or freezing of pork for a period of time can kill these parasites. This is still recommended today even for inspected meat.

Chemical Food Poisoning

There are many foods in the natural state which contain toxins. Manioca and soybeans are foods that contain toxins which are destroyed through processing. Many species of mushrooms as well as some species of fish contain deadly poisons. What is important to know is which foods are poisonous. Some of these will be discussed in Chapter 20. It should be noted that many plants contain various chemicals which are extracted for use as drugs. If taken in large doses, death could occur.

Salmonella

The Center for Disease Control in Atlanta, Georgia, run by the Department of Health, Education and Welfare, attempts to collect data on food poisoning throughout the United States. Overall, there are approximately 2 million cases of food poisoning reported every year. Many illnesses that are commonly diagnosed as the *24-hr flu* are in reality food poisoning. Approximately another 200 million cases of food poisonings probably occur every year, though they are not reported because they do not recognize it as food poisoning.

Salmonellosis was very common a few years ago. It is on the decline at the present time, although it still accounts for 3% of all reported cases of poisoning. The major symptoms of salmonellosis are vomiting, diarrhea, and fever. The salmonella organism grows only in the large intestine of man and animals unless it gets into a food supply which is high in protein, where it can grow if the temperature is kept high (80 to 100°F). Over 70% of all salmonellosis cases are the result of eating contaminated meats and poultry. One previously common carrier was *Salmonella typhi*, which is the organism causing typhoid fever and is transmitted in water contaminated by sewage. The food-related organism is *Salmonella typhimurium* which is associated many times with processed meats due to unsanitary conditions in the slaughter house. Under poor conditions, fecal matter from the intestines of diseased animals

contaminates the edible meat, causing a severe illness when
consumed. The organisms grow rapidly in the intestine of
man and somehow cause the severe reactions. Symptoms are
usually not evident until about 7 to 72 hr after eating and can
last about 48 hr with severe dehydration. Young children and
elderly people, having less resistance, are severely affected
by salmonellosis. In many cases they die.

Good sanitation is the primary method for preventing food
poisoning from *Salmonella*. Hands should always be washed
when preparing foods. If the food is cooked properly the organism is killed because it cannot survive high heat. Usually
what happens, however, is that a contaminated roast is cut
up on a board first, and then roasted; the board, if used again
before washing, will recontaminate the roast or other food
when sliced. Sanitation thus is the real problem.

Clostridium perfringens

Food poisoning from the *Clostridium perfringens* bacteria
is one of the most common forms of food poisoning. Symptoms
of this food poisoning are mild cramps and diarrhea occurring
from 4 to 22 hr after eating, similar to the symptoms for the
24-hr flu. It is usually contracted from meats, eggs, gravies,
and other protein foods. This organism has two stages: a live
growing cell and a stagnant spore state and is usually present
on all foods, including meats. The way the toxin is produced is
unusual. Cooking roast beef in an oven will kill the growing
cells, but it does not kill the spores since they are heat-resistant. If the roast is immediately cooled there is no problem;
but holding the meat for a long time at serving temperature,
as is the case in many homes and restaurants, will activate
the spores and cells will grow again to high numbers. Once
inside the intestine, the conditions cause spores to form again,
with the production of a toxin. Sanitation is important in the
prevention of this disease; still more important is rapid cooling
of meats and gravies if they have to be held for any time, or
holding roasts at 150°F for serving purposes to inactivate the
Cl. perfringens microorganism. Unfortunately, holding at
the higher temperature destroys nutrients, so cooling is pref-
erable. This disease is especially prevalent because of improperly handled food in restaurants. A common home practice

is also responsible—letting meat cool down before refrigeration. Most meats and gravies should be refrigerated as soon as possible after serving or cooking.

Staphylococcus

Another very common food poisoning is due to the *Staphylococcus* organism. This poisoning is caused by a toxic chemical that the organism produces as it grows. Symptoms manifest themselves within 2 to 4 hr after consumption of the contaminated food. It is most commonly associated with cream pastries and with tuna salad, chicken salad, and similar mixtures, especially salads made for picnics. This organism is present on all parts of the human body. The myth that mayonnaise causes this food poisoning is common, but is simply not true. The actual cause is unsanitary food preparation: people often do not clean their hands before making such salad mixes by hand. Usually because of the salt or sugar added to the mix, conditions are set up to allow growth, especially if the food is held out in the sun unrefrigerated. Sanitation and refrigeration are important for preventing the growth of the *Staphylococcus* since in this case, the toxin is heat-resistant so that cooking does not destroy the toxin.

Botulism

Clostridium botulinum is an organism which can grow in underprocessed canned foods in which the spores are not killed. When they grow, a toxin is produced which is very deadly, as discussed in Chapter 13. Botulism poisoning symptoms occur as late as 7 days after the ingestion of the toxin. Botulism poisoning is usually 50% fatal. Symptoms including double vision and muscular paralysis occur. Death results as a failure of nerve transmission resulting in the inability to breathe and suffocation. The simple procedure of heating the canned food before consumption would prevent the poisoning, since the toxin is heat-sensitive. Many canned foods such as tomatoes, juices and pickled produce are safe, since the organism cannot grow in acid. The major way to prevent this disease is to not eat food from smelly, damaged or bulging cans and to ensure proper processing.

Summary

In terms of numbers of cases of food poisoning that have been reported over the last 5 years, 5 out of 6 have occurred as a result of improper preparation and/or handling of foods in homes, schools, restaurants and other food-service estab lishments. Only 1 out of 6 incidents of food poisoning is due to mishandling in the manufacturing process in the food industry. Unfortunately, since the industry prepares foods in bulk quantities, many more people could be infected by their mistakes, so that precaution in processing is the rule. In industry sanitary techniques require workers to wear gloves and hair nets. Food services usually have the same requirements, but much negligence is found in this area. Following good sanitary practices would certainly reduce illnesses in the United States resulting from food poisoning.

CHAPTER 19

Food Regulations and Legislation

History of the Food and Drug Administration

There were no federal food laws in the United States prior to the 1900's. At that time food companies could add anything they chose to their food products. Many illnesses probably occurred from the addition of untested chemicals to the food supply. Vast quantities of chalk were added to milk to stretch out milk sales. Adding chalk to bread to mask dirty flour was also a common practice. Mixing lard with butter was also done.

Harvey Wiley, U.S. Director of Agriculture in 1902, set up a group to study the problems in the food supply which became known as Wiley's Poison Squad. It was made up of volunteers who would go out to various stores and suppliers, purchase foods, bring them back to department headquarters, and analyze and taste them to see if anything was wrong. Testing the foods by eating them was not the best or safest method for determining their safety, but at that time no procedures had been established for testing toxicity. Wiley found many things wrong and let the information out to the public.

At about the same time the Poison Squad went into effect, Upton Sinclair wrote a book, *The Jungle,* dealing with the horrid, unsanitary conditions of the Chicago stockyards and the meat processors. After the publication of that book many foreign countries banned the importation of U.S. beef. In 1906 pressure from various consumers on the legislature resulted in the passage of the *Pure Food and Drug Act and the Meat Inspection Act* under the authority of the USDA (United States Department of Agriculture). This act required that the food supply in interstate commerce was to be safe and that any chemical added to foods should be safe and have a useful purpose. No provisions, penalties, or authorizations were given to any governmental agency other than the right to inspect food plants and publish the results of investigations of food products. As a result of the strong pressure applied by lobbyists for several food companies, however, it was left up to the government to prove the fault of the food manufacturer. Because of this, the act was virtually ineffective since there were no powers of enforcement.

In 1931 the Food and Drug Administration (FDA) was formed under the USDA to administer the law. The FDA was ineffective until 1938, at which time the *Food Drug and Cosmetic Act of 1938* gave the FDA the power to fine and imprison violators of the laws based on the misbranding and adulteration of foods. The provisions of this act will be discussed in the next section. It was still up to the government to investigate and prosecute the violators, and the burden of proof was still on the government.

Much bickering about the location of the FDA within the Department of Agriculture finally resulted in the relocation of the FDA in 1953 to include it within the Department of Health, Education and Welfare. However, meat inspection remained under the jurisdiction of the USDA. Today it is still possible that several different governmental agencies all having authority and regulatory power can control the production, handling, and marketing of a single food item. This obviously can create problems as to which law takes precedence.

In 1954 a pesticide amendment was added to the *Food Drug and Cosmetic Act* with regard to the amount of pesticides that could be left on crops once they entered the market. This was added due to the occurrence of an extensive gypsy moth blight in New York and Connecticut in 1953. The USDA decided to eliminate the gypsy moths by spraying DDT. They contracted local people who owned small planes, shipped them many 100 lb bags of DDT, and told the pilots to spray it over designated infected areas, which included residential areas. This created much opposition by home owners who had large doses of DDT dropped in their yards. This led to congressional pressure and in 1954 the pesticides amendment that was enacted stated that there was to be a maximum tolerance level of various pesticides in final food products. In some cases the tolerance level was set at *zero*, that is, no pesticides could be present. This obviously would change as analytical techniques for the pesticides improved and lower levels could be detected.

In 1957 the USDA added the *Poultry Inspection Act* to its

jurisdiction. Prior to that time, the advent of central locations
for the raising of fryer and broiler chickens near big cities
was occurring. Before shipping, some poultry raisers were
feeding binding agents to chickens which caused them to retain
water. This increased their weight at the time of sale. This
act specified what was legal to feed to a chicken and outlined
the practices that were necessary to maintain good sanitation
in the poultry plant.

Probably the most significant food legislation occurred in
1958 when the *Food Additive Amendment* was added to the
original *Food Drug and Cosmetic Act.* The significance of this
act was several fold. First, it defined what a food additive
was. Secondly, the responsibility for proving the safety and
efficacy of an additive was put on the food company trying to
introduce it, rather than on the government. The *Delaney
Clause,* which was a rider attached to this act, controlled
the addition of carcinogenic additives to food. It was made a
law that no chemicals which could cause cancer in man or
animals could be added to foods. This will be discussed in
Chapter 20.

In 1960 other amendments were added concerning color
additives. They specified that all coloring agents had to be
tested and certified by the government before they could be
used in foods.

In 1966 the *Fair Packaging and Labeling Act* was passed
giving power to regulate advertising on all packaged items,
including foods. The jurisdiction for this with respect to foods,
however, was put under the Federal Trade Commission (FTC)
rather than under the FDA. This act also covers advertising
on radio and television. Again, this points out some of the
jurisdictional problems of who has control.

In 1973 nutritional labeling rules were placed on foods to
help educate the consumer about nutritional values. These
rules state what can be claimed about the nutritional value of
a food. This helps to prevent erroneous or exaggerated claims
for natural compounds present in foods which have been claimed
to have magic powers. In addition, in 1973 the Supreme Court
affirmed the right of the FDA to take out of the food supply
any drug or chemical which is not effective for the job for
which it was intended. The FDA also emphasized at that time
that it was going to get tough with any plant that produces food

under unsanitary conditions to the point of giving prison sentences to company executives.

Provisions of the Pure Food and Drug Act

Food Adulteration.—Food adulteration is defined as the intentional or unintentional addition of any poisonous or deleterious substance to food. This not only applies to actual food additives, but also to items that are not specifically an intentional chemical additive. For instance, if *Clostridium botulinum* or any other pathogen was found to grow in canned foods it would be considered to be a poisonous substance. Therefore, it would be within the power of the government to seize the food, destroy it, and impose penalties. The contamination due to rat feces in food because of mishandling or poor sanitation is also considered to be food adulteration. Levels of ingredients stated on a package found to be in excess or below the stated or required percentage can effect seizure of the food product. For example, if the amount of egg in mayonnaise is below the standard, the food is considered to be adulterated. Foods that contain levels of filth such as insect fragments, dirt, etc., above the tolerances allowable are considered to be adulterated. One of the tenets of food processing is that if food is unacceptable at the initial stages of processing, further processing is not going to improve it. This prevents manufacturers from processing diseased animals or decayed food. Extraction of a valuable vitamin is also considered to be food adulteration. Concealment of damage to food by the use of food additives is also against the law and is considered to be adulteration.

In 1972 the FDA published filth guidelines stating levels of filth that are acceptable in foods. For example, in 3 oz of peanut butter, up to 50 insect fragments and two rodent hairs are allowed, since this occurs in the raw nuts themselves and is hard to prevent unless excessively costly procedures are used. Similarly, vegetables like broccoli can contain up to 60 insect fragments for the same reasons. These guidelines also prevent manufacturers from mixing clean and unclean batches of food to arrive at tolerance levels for the unacceptable batch. Good manufacturing practices by companies would keep the levels well below the tolerances, since they would be following sanitary procedures.

Unsanitary practices in production are also included in food adulteration legislation. In the past the low number of food inspectors who work for the FDA has made adequate inspection of all food plants almost impossible. Because of consumer pressures, the FDA budget has been increased so that additional inspectors could be hired. In addition, a new code called the GMP (Good Manufacturing Practices) has been set up by the FDA for companies that are capable of self-policing. They submit the outline of their food processing and sanitation programs for approval. The larger food-processing companies are more capable of self-policing than smaller companies, and have found this procedure to be useful in ensuring clean, high-quality food to the consumer. In 1973 Congress also acted on a bill to require all food companies to register with the FDA. Many food companies are virtually unknown, and some extremely small companies are never found by the FDA.

Misbranding.—False labeling is the most obvious indiscretion listed under misbranding. For example, a nutrition claim cannot be made for a non-essential amino acid. Substitution is also listed under misbranding violations. An example of substitution would be the substitution of margarine for butter, which occurred relatively frequently when margarine was first manufactured. Package deception in terms of fill of containers is clarified by statements on packages saying that settling may occur, etc.; however, a reasonable-size package must be used or a certain fill is necessary.

Standards of identity are one of the most controversial areas in food legislation. They are useful in defining how many peanuts should be in peanut butter or how much fruit should be in a jam, since they prevent companies from using lesser amounts. However, the addition of lysine to white bread is prohibited even though the addition would improve protein quality because this practice is not in the standards. A new standard has to be applied for. A similar problem arose in adding protein to pasta to increase protein quality. To get around the standard, a special allowance was made by the FDA. This will be more common in the future if nutritional value of a food can be upgraded by the addition of an ingredient.

Other Regulatory Agencies

The USDA is second in power to the FDA in food-quality regulation. The USDA is responsible for the inspection, at the processing and slaughtering level, of all meat and poultry that go through interstate shipment. These inspectors check for diseased animals as well as for plant sanitation. New laws require that state guidelines for inspection be equal to the USDA standards. In many cases the USDA has taken over intrastate inspection as well (meats slaughtered and used within the state's boundaries). The USDA also sets guidelines with respect to plant construction, personal hygiene, and meat food composition.

The grading of beef is a service paid for by the food companies and done by the USDA. Grading lists beef in categories: prime, choice, good, standard, commercial, utility, cutter, and canner. This benefits the consumer in knowing what quality meat he is buying. Descriptions of meat cuts are also a new development currently being formulated by the USDA to eliminate the many varied names for the same kinds of meats. This again would benefit the consumer. The USDA also grades vegetables, fruits, bread, and dairy products as a service to food companies.

The U.S. Public Health Service is responsible for several areas of food regulations: water standards and control of all foods served on planes, trains, and buses. They also will voluntarily, if requested, inspect milk for certification as raw milk and certify that shellfish come from non-polluted water.

The National Marine and Fisheries Bureau of the U.S. Department of Commerce is responsible for quality assurance in fish processing. The Occupational Safety and Health Administration (OSHA) is responsible for setting safety regulations in food-processing plants. Problems have been created between safety standards which may allow unsanitary conditions and food regulations which might allow a possible unsafe condition. This is evident, for example, in a required blade guard over a band saw used to cut meat which might allow organisms to grow on it. Some of the Federal agencies such as the Environmental Protection Agency (EPA) also regulate pesticide occurrence in foods to varying degrees. Pesticides are covered

by the FDA under adulteration, under the USDA, and also tolerance levels have been set by the EPA.

The U.S. Department of the Treasury governs all the regulations concerning the production and sales of wines, beers,
and liquors. The Federal Trade Commission regulates labels
and advertising. Some confusion exists about the actions and
interactions of the various regulatory agencies which hopefully
will be solved in the future without causing detriment to the
consumer.

Testing of Food Additives

Food Additives Amendment

In 1958 the Food Additives Amendment was passed placing the responsibility for proving the safety and efficacy of a food additive on the company interested in introducing the additive into the food supply. A food additive is anything added to a food intentionally to improve the quality, nutrient value, texture or shelf life of the food. The law also covers any chemical which through processing or storage might migrate into food unintentionally. Calcium propionate is an intentional additive added to bread to prevent mold growth and thus improve shelf life of the product. Examples of unintentional additives are: glycerine (a chemical added to plastic packaging films to impart softness) which could migrate from a polyethylene packaging film, migration of cleaning residues from the processing machine's surface, and pesticides which introduced on the farm were not cleaned off in processing.

From a legal standpoint all food additives are toxic at some level of consumption. They must, therefore, be tested before they can be used in a food. This toxicity establishes the *risk/ benefit* ratio. The use of each additive causes some risk to the person consuming it. Hopefully, by the procedures used for testing the chemical, the risk can be established and the tolerance level can be set. The benefit is the increased quality, nutritional value, shelf-life, etc. imparted to the food. Everyone should be made aware of the risk/benefit ratio of the additives in the foods they consume. Standard procedures for testing additives for safety are not formalized by law; however, the government will not approve an additive unless a certain protocol is used. Above all, the additive must be safe and effective.

The *Delaney Clause* of the *Food Drug and Cosmetic Act* states that any substance which, when fed to either man or animals, is found to induce cancer, or as the result of appropriate testing procedures for the evaluation of safety of additives also induces cancer, is to be banned from the food supply. This means that there is a zero tolerance level for additives that do not pass these criteria. This law may not be 100% accurate for all additives, but it does prevent the addition of carcinogenic chemicals to the food supply. The interpretation of the tests used has created much controversy.

GRAS (Generally Recognized as Safe) Chemicals

GRAS chemical additives are considered to be harmless when added to the food supply under normal manufacturing processes. They are nontoxic under normal use (anything ingested in high enough levels can cause death, including water). If a manufacturer was going to make a beef stew, the potatoes and carrots could be considered additives, but would be included on the GRAS list since they are safe to use in a normal diet.

The GRAS list was composed in 1958 at the request of the FDA by about 300 scientists who submitted the names of materials that could be classified as GRAS. Because some of these substances were subsequently found to have not been properly tested, the FDA rewrote the definitions of the list in 1973 and began examining all the chemicals on it for re-affirmation of their safety.

The first category on the new GRAS list is *foods of natural biological origin* consumed for nutritive purposes and used without detrimental effect prior to 1958. For example, the natural food components of the beef stew previously mentioned would be included under this heading on the GRAS list. *Foods modified by conventional processing and used prior to 1958* is a second category on the GRAS list. The modification of starches to make a better gel is an example of this latter category as well as is the modification of flour and gelatin for similar purposes.

Everything on the GRAS list other than the two categories listed above is currently under re-examination, scrutiny, and possible testing for safety and efficacy. These include *foods or chemicals modified by new processes since 1958* and foods which have been altered by breeding or genetic selection. An example of the latter category is the new variety of tomato that can be mechanically harvested due to a firmer consistency. The FDA is concerned with the nutritional quality of the tomato in comparison to past norms. Some tests indicate that there is 30% less vitamin C in this new variety of tomatoes than is found in regular tomatoes. It is also not known whether this breeding would cause toxic chemicals to form.

Another class of chemicals on the GRAS list which is being examined is the category including *substances which are of biological origin but are not used for nutritive purposes*. Coffee, tea, salt, and MSG (monosodium glutamate) are items in this category. Coffee under certain testing procedures has been shown to cause chromosome destruction (undesirable genetic changes in rats) but it will probably be included on the approved GRAS list due to its widespread use and acceptance for hundreds of years.

The remaining category on the GRAS list under examination consists of the various kinds of *synthetic chemicals in use in the food industry* which are considered to be nontoxic but should be retested or reaffirmed. Examples are many of the approved flavoring agents and colors. Once all these chemicals are reviewed they will either remain on the GRAS list or become a regulated food additive.

The overall view of the food additives law thus places additives in two groups: (1) regulated food additives which are toxic at low doses and (2) GRAS list chemicals which are not toxic under normal use. The former additives have a regulation as to the amount that can be used because they can be toxic to humans if too high a dose is used. The procedures for determining the safe level will be discussed below.

Introducing a Food Additive into the Market

Before a food company can introduce a new chemical into the market 3 to 4 years of research would be necessary at a probable cost of between $0.5 to $3 million. This means a large but necessary financial burden on a company. Because of this cost and time the likelihood that very many new food additives will be introduced into the food supply in the near future is small.

The first step in the quest for an additive is to determine if a *need* exists in a current food product to improve its quality, shelf-life, etc. The primary prerequisite for seeking an additive to solve the problem is lack of processing techniques

capable of doing the job. The improvement may be accomplished
in several ways. Chemicals already utilized by the food industry would be one alternative. A search, therefore, can be
made of an already approved additive that would be effective.
A chemical that is available but has not been used in the food
market is another choice. This is more difficult, since the
biological safety of this chemical may have not been proved.
A third resource could be the chemistry department of a company that might be able to synthesize a new chemical based
on the properties needed to solve the problem. Again, toxicity
would have to be determined. Simultaneously, it is necessary
to convince the management of the company that it would be
economically feasible to go ahead. If the improved market
position of the company is not going to bring much more profit,
it may not be worth the high cost of testing and getting approval
of the additive.

The testing that would result from a decision to begin work
on the use of a new additive is lengthy. The first step in the
testing is to prove the efficacy of the additive, i.e., that it
is suitable for the job intended, such as increasing shelf-life.
Levels of consumption of the additive in a normal diet (mg/kg
of body weight) would have to be determined based on the effectiveness level of the additive needed to improve the food.
A method of analysis for determining the presence of the chemical in the product also must be developed.

The most difficult step is to test the chemical for toxicity.
If an additive is already used in foods this may not be necessary. Biological testing could require up to 3 years of research
to prove safety. Three specific kinds of toxicity tests are
generally required: acute, subacute, and chronic.

The acute toxicity test utilizes two species of animals, usually rats and dogs. The animals are given single doses of the
chemical by injection into the blood stream or by feeding.
Dosages are increased until the dose level is found which kills
50% of the animals within one week after injection or feeding.
This dose is called the LD_{50} (lethal dose for 50% of the animals). The LD_{50} is computed in terms of mg of the chemical
per kg of body weight and is compared with the effectiveness
levels needed in the food product. Obviously, if the LD_{50} level
was less than the effectiveness level of the chemical, it could
not be utilized in the product.

The next step is to test at subacute toxicity levels. Animals of two or more species are fed at levels of the chemical much lower than the LD_{50} level every day for 90 days. Usually 3 dose levels are used. The major evaluation in this study is the observation of the state of health of the animals. The animals are given physical examinations including weight measurements and chemical analyses of blood and urine. At the end of the study an autopsy is performed on each animal to determine if any changes in the organs have occurred. All the tests are aimed at finding a level of the chemical that causes a minimum biochemical or physiological change. This level is again determined in mg/kg of body weight. The number is then divided by 100 to set the maximum acceptable level for human consumption. At the present time there is no better method for determining the safety of a chemical for humans than using animals. The 100 times safety divisor has not been proved to be totally accurate. The most critical toxicological research currently under way at the present time deals with establishing a better method of determining a safety factor. In some cases, it may be either larger or smaller than 100. Again, this level should be below the needed effectiveness level of the chemical.

The final test is a chronic toxicity test procedure which requires 3 years of feeding studies to determine harmful effects. Two species of animals (rats and dogs) are used with a minimum of 25 each of females and males for both the test group and the control group. Three years is chosen so that several generations of the test group can be studied. Examination of the offspring for birth defects is very important. Levels of the chemical below the minimum physiological response level are administered daily with physical and clinical examinations occurring every 3 to 6 months. The usual levels picked are at 10 and 50 times the safety level for humans in mg/kg of body weight. Examination of the animal during autopsy for any tumors that might be cancerous is of great importance. This is done to comply with the Delaney Clause. Interpretation of the results, however, has led to much controversy. If the studies indicate a higher incidence of cancer in the test diet, the additive is not allowed; however, some tests have shown that even the controls have high levels of cancerous tumors. Several generations are carried through the experiment so that birth defects and/or abnormal litter size can be examined. Again, any adverse effect would prevent use of the additive.

A question as to the need and advisability of better testing programs for indicating a cancer-causing chemical is under discussion at the present time by various government and private organizations. It is possible to utilize different kinds of tests to prove that almost anything can provoke the generation of tumors. Sugar and salt when injected under the skin have been shown to produce tumors. Only if the tumor metastasizes (releases cells which cause tumors in other parts of the body) is the chemical causing the tumor considered to be cancerous, since such tumors are malignant. A rapid biological detection test for chemicals that would apply to man is needed.

Besides testing for cancer, the FDA is also interested in whether the chemicals cause birth defects or mutations. Specific tests may also be required to ensure acceptance of an additive. Some of these will be discussed later.

After a chemical additive has been put through all the tests and is found to be safe and effective, the food company petitions the FDA for acceptance. The FDA in turn publishes the information about the new additive in the *Federal Register* if it is felt that the tests done were adequate to ensure safety. Over 80% of petitions submitted to the FDA are rejected on the basis of insufficient data. The FDA also establishes the permissible levels that can be used (regulated food additive). At this point, any person in the country can write to the FDA to express an opinion about the published additive. Public response within a 90-day period may affect the acceptance of the chemical into the market to the point of requiring further testing. Overall, the testing procedures, time periods, expense involved, and legal processes greatly restrict the addition of new additives into the market. If all goes well the additive can be used. Hopefully, new and better procedures subsequently developed will verify the safety of the chemical additive. In some cases, however, approved chemicals, such as cyclamates, have been found to be carcinogenic and have had to be removed from the food supply.

Mutagenic Chemicals

Mutagenic chemicals are those which can cause anything from a very minor mutation that may be undetectable to those which cause cancer or birth defects. If minor, the mutagenic and carcinogenic effects may take as long as 20 to 30 years to become evident in humans. From an evolutionary aspect those animals which mutated were the ones who survived because they were able to adapt to a new environment. One theory is that additives could be beneficial from the adaptive standpoint since man may become resistant to detrimental environments. However, the risk involved prevents us from testing this theory. Many generations or a very large population are necessary to test for a minor mutagenic effect, so the result is more statistical, that is, one can only say that a chemical may be mutagenic to some degree of probability. A teratogenic chemical is very obvious since it causes visible birth defects such as were caused by thalidomide.

Microorganisms, such as certain bacteria, are most commonly used for testing for mutagenic effects, since the metabolic pathways, structures and genetic makeup are completely mapped. Since microbes grow rapidly and produce many generations, the mutagenic effect can be observed better. The chemical in question is introduced into the growth medium of these organisms. The changes, if any, in metabolism and genetic material of the cell are examined. The validity of such tests is questioned when the results are compared to humans, because most chemicals ingested and absorbed through the small intestine in humans pass through the liver first. The liver has many mechanisms for detoxifying chemicals, rendering them harmless to the body. They are then excreted in the urine. Bacteria do not have this property.

Human tissue cultures are also utilized for studying mutagenic effects. These are human placental cells grown in special test tubes. They are observed for mutagenic effects with the introduction of the chemical being tested in much the same way as for bacteria. Similarly, the effects of the liver are not accounted for in these tests.

A more complicated test developed during the early 1970's called the *Host Mediated Assay* eliminates the discrepancies caused by the absence of a liver. In this test, bacteria cultures are injected into the lining between the lungs and the skin of a dog. The bacteria are exposed to the blood and lymph system of the dog and can grow without harming the dog. The chemical being tested is fed in a large dose to the animal. In this manner the bacteria are exposed to the chemical via the normal digestive functions and liver action of the dog. After ingestion of the chemical, some of the bacteria are removed at 4-hr intervals over a week's time. The bacteria are then grown in cultures to determine if mutations have occurred.

The *Dominant Lethal Test* is a test in which male rats have the chemical in question fed to them or injected into them. Female rats are then bred with these males. Halfway through pregnancy the female is sacrificed and the fetuses are examined for any genetic changes. Large changes are the only ones that are evident, although it is possible to see if any fetuses have died and been reabsorbed, since a scar will be evident on the wall of the uterus. It is presumed that if this occurred, a minor mutation took place which caused the fetus to be rejected by the mother.

At the present time some people are trying to introduce into the legislature an addition to the Delaney Clause that would state that any chemicals which can be considered to be mutagenic should also be banned from the food supply. This may be a good idea but none of the test procedures can be applied with reliability to man.

Problem Chemical Additives

Some chemicals that have been in the diet but have been removed from the market because of the problems they caused are discussed below.

DES (diethylstilbesterol) is a synthetic growth hormone which was used in animal feeds for beef cattle for purposes of increasing the feed efficiency of the animal. The animal on DES could convert a higher percentage of its feed into protein. When it became evident that an unusually large number of girls between the ages of 18 to 20 developed cervical cancer, it came to light that the mothers of these girls had all had problems becoming pregnant. They had been given large doses of DES as a fertility drug to assist them in becoming pregnant. It was assumed that the cancer was caused by the DES, a slow mutation taking place.

The FDA went to work checking animals for the presence of DES in meat. Approximately 2 samples in 10,000 showed evidence of this chemical. However, since there was a zero tolerance level allowed because of the carcinogenic effects, the use of DES in animal feed was banned to some degree. Tests utilized at that time indicated that approximately 10 days after taking the animals off the DES, no evidence of it appeared in the tissue of the animal.

It was decided therefore that feed containing DES should be withdrawn from the animals 10 days prior to slaughter. Due to the failure to comply with this 10-day ruling by some unknowledgeable or unscrupulous farmers, the FDA has *temporarily* banned the use of DES.

FDC Red #2 was a coloring agent used in lipstick, animal foods, beverages and candies. It was removed from the provisional color list in 1976 thus effectively banning its use because some Russian studies in 1970 showed carcinogenicity and early fetal deaths in rats. The FDA realized these were imperfect studies and did their own which were also botched up. However, because of possible political pressure and expediency on the side of safety, the FDA delisted the coloring agent.

Violet #1 was used until the spring of 1973 for stamping the grades of meat onto beef carcasses. Some Japanese studies showed Violet #1 fed at 5% of the diet to be carcinogenic and it has been removed from the market. However, re-examination of the Japanese data showed that their study was done poorly. Most of the animals contracted pneumonia and were given simultaneously large doses of antibiotics. Most of the animals died. The results showing detrimental effects of Violet #1 were based on only a few rats that survived the pneumonia.

Saccharin was tested for toxicity in 1966 in studies done with mixtures of cyclamate and saccharin on rats. Pellets of this mixture were implanted in the bladders of rats. Higher incidences of tumors were noted with the rats subjected to implantation. From these studies, it was decided that cyclamates caused the tumors rather than saccharin. This was further substantiated by the fact that a metabolic product of cyclamates was found to be carcinogenic. New studies question this assumption. Saccharin is now also under investigation since some studies also question its safety.

Nitrite is utilized in the curing of meats like bacon, ham, and hot dogs to reduce the amount of heat necessary to preserve the food, to color the meat pink, and to add the meat-cured flavor. It has been found that under high temperatures or high acid conditions the nitrites can react with certain amino acids forming compounds known as nitrosamines. Nitrosamines are considered to be one of the most potent carcinogenic substances known to man. It is felt that nitrosamines can be formed within the highly acid conditions of the stomach by eating meat products which contain nitrites. Furthermore, it is hypothesized that increases of stomach or colon cancer will result. Bacon is very suspect since it contains an amino acid in high concentration that can react with nitrite during frying to produce the carcinogen. Most bacon samples tested show a trace amount (in parts per billion) of the nitrosamines. Whether this would be a problem in the normal diet is not known, but is currently under test. Statistical analysis of populations eating large quantities of nitrite-cured meat correlate with high percentages of cancer. The FDA will probably ban the use of nitrite unless a way to prevent its reaction is found. This will have serious implications for farmers who grow both pigs and corn and may affect the economy of the United States drastically. Again, the risk/benefit question must be answered.

Tests involving excess levels of *monosodium glutamate* (MSG), a flavor enhancer, in the diets of immature rats have shown that it might cause tissue damage to the brain. MSG was used in baby food, but since has been removed because its original purpose was to make the food appeal to mothers rather than to babies. Some people are also sensitive to MSG and have a condition known as the Chinese Restaurant Syndrome. If they eat soup at a restaurant that has a high level of MSG, they get a severe headache and become dizzy. However, this chemical is essentially the salt of a natural amino acid which has not been found to be toxic by regular tests, and is thus allowed.

Problems in Additive-Food Interactions

Variability of the diet makes it difficult to evaluate the effects of various chemicals as do physical size and age differences.

For example, babies, and older people may be more sensitive to a chemical than middle-aged persons. Diseases existing at the same time as the ingestion of chemicals could cause the chemical to react in a different manner. Testing for this variable is difficult or impossible. Some people may eat an abnormally excessive amount of one food and have some adverse effect. This has happened in the case of one person who ate a large amount of swordfish every day and developed minor mercury poisoning.

Data about the interactions between the various food chemicals are also absent. All chemicals used in foods are usually tested individually, but few tests have been done to show the interactions among a combination of these chemical additives. Ingestion of chemical additives during pregnancy and their effect on the unborn child are also risks which may not become evident in the chronic toxicity test.

Data on the interactions of the various chemical additives with prescription and over-the-counter drugs are not available. Some drug packages state that alcohol should not be consumed while the person is using the drug. This is due to interactions between the chemicals. Likewise, there are some tranquilizers which can produce deleterious effects if certain foods are eaten. They suppress an enzyme in the liver which detoxifies certain natural chemicals that are found in bananas, wine, beer, yogurt, and certain cheeses. Use of these foods can lead to death if the wrong combination is used. Unfortunately, not enough doctors are aware of this. Antacids will irreversibly bind calcium and iron, cutting down on the absorption of these important nutrients from the small intestine.

The use of oral contraceptives by women seems to indicate the need for increased amounts of folic acid in their diet. The reasons are not clear. Green leafy vegetables are the best sources of folic acid. A problem can exist in that young women who use oral contraceptives may not like to eat vegetables.

These facts would lead one to believe that all additives can be detrimental, but many foods are also harmful under certain conditions. Alcohol is a primary example of a naturally occurring harmful food or drug. Psychological problems and physical problems including damage to the liver and kidney may result from the intake of high levels of alcohol over a long period of time.

Coffee and tea contain caffein which can be proved to be mutagenic to microbes under the specific test conditions previously outlined.

Cabbage, cauliflower, and Brussels sprouts, when consumed in large quantities, can suppress the uptake of iodine by the thyroid because of a chemical they contain. Unrefined oils can contain carcinogenic compounds which are removed in normal refining processes. Their use should be limited. Honey can also be toxic when manufactured from undesirable plants. Toxic honey is produced by many bees in Southern Greece and Italy.

Various kinds of beans can cause diseases. Many of these diseases are found among poor desert populations. Many times under drought conditions plants such as chick peas are the only ones able to survive and are consumed in large quanties. The chick peas contain a chemical which causes muscular weakness and can lead to death. Uncooked soybeans contain chemicals that prevent protein digestion and can destroy red blood cells.

Nutmeg can also be lethal in large quantities. The same is true of green potatoes. The green color is characteristic of the presence of an alkaloid called solanine. It has been responsible for the deaths of several people consuming an excess of green potatoes.

Rhubarb and spinach contain oxalic acid. When consumed in excess, this binds the iron preventing absorption within the body. Some mushrooms and fish livers are poisonous.

Manioca is a plant that is the seventh largest consumed food in the world. We know it in the refined form as tapioca. It is used mainly in tropical countries by developing populations. Manioca is a root-type food that, because of the presence of hydrogen cyanide, would be fatal if cooked and eaten directly. However, preparation procedures have been developed to make it safe for consumption by washing and extracting.

Summary

It should be realized that anything consumed in excess can be harmful. It is not the chemical that is harmful, but the dose ingested that causes the harm. We must understand the risks involved in eating certain additives and the benefits they give us. As an example, much bread produced centrally would mold rapidly if calcium propionate was not added. Calcium propionate is toxic at some level to humans; that is the risk. The benefit is increased shelf-life and reduced waste. Bread would mold in 3 days without the mold inhibitor as compared to 10 days with it. This would be an economic loss to the country as a whole. Hopefully, in the future we will learn more about the risk/benefit ratio of all foods we consume.

Chemist Using Gas Chromatography to Detect Pesticide Residues

CHAPTER 21

The United States Diet

General Problems

The United States is one of the most affluent countries in the world, yet problems with diet and food consumption still exist. Malnutrition can be found in some parts of the country. Obesity may affect as much as 20% of the population. Fad diets and other special diets are constantly being tried by people with little knowledge of nutrition in hope of some miraculous weight loss, weight gain, or disease cure. Various scientific groups argue over the validity of diet change with respect to heart and artery disease. Hopefully, better research and education will solve some of these problems.

Malnutrition

Much of the malnutrition found in the United States is limited to poverty areas where the problems are both lack of money and lack of education as to how to use the money available to choose a proper diet. However, malnutrition is not confined to poor people. The change in life style to the rapid pace of today has virtually eliminated breakfast from the diets of many. The proliferation of snack foods helps to detract from eating a balanced diet even when money is available. Aged people find it hard to get around so just don't shop for food as much. They also may not be able to eat the same things as they did when they were younger.

All these problems were pointed out when the Ten State Nutrition Survey was conducted by the U.S. Department of Health, Education and Welfare between 1968 and 1970. Some of the results found are summarized in Table 21.1. As seen, high percentages of the population were found that consumed various nutrients below the RDA. However, as pointed out, the RDA is set high. What is of consequence is the number below one-half of the RDA; 1% of the population translates into over 250,000 people, which is a large number indeed. A survey of health data in 1967 found, however, that severe vitamin deficiencies

TABLE 21.1
RESULTS OF TEN-STATE NUTRITION SURVEY

Nutrient	% of Population Below RDA	% of Population Below 1/2 RDA
Calcium	56	8
Iron	58	3
Vitamin A	30	5
Vitamin B$_1$	50	2
Vitamin B$_2$	38	4
Niacin	40	1
Vitamin C	52	10

were a very small problem. Only 13 cases of pellagra were reported, 10 cases of rickets, no scurvy, and almost no goiter. In many cases, education was all that was needed to alleviate the deficiencies. It is surprising to note that in 1970 vitamin C was found to be below 1/2 the RDA in 10% of the population surveyed. This shows the trend toward reduced consumption of fruits and vegetables. Even in school lunch programs where vegetables, fruits and salads are served, a survey of consumption shows that the children leave 1/2 the vegetables, 1/3 the fruit, and the salad is not usually eaten.

Another interesting fact was that in 1955, when a similar survey was made, about 15% of households had poor diets and 60% had good nutritionally balanced diets. However, in 1965 poor diets were found in 20% of families and good diets in only 50%. Hopefully, the trend is reversing as a result of better education but no data exist to prove it. Money is not the answer since in 1965, 10% of the poor diets were found in families in the top income bracket.

Consumption Patterns

Table 21.2 shows the change in consumption patterns between 1950 and 1972. An examination of the Table shows that we have increased meat and poultry consumption enormously. This could cause problems with respect to liver and kidney damage if too much protein is consumed. We eat less eggs and dairy products probably because of the heart disease and cholesterol

TABLE 21.2
U.S.A. — CONSUMPTION DATA

Food	Lb/Person/Yr 1950	1972	% Change
Meats	145	189	+31
Fish	11.8	11.5	−2.5
Eggs	389	315	−19
Chicken/turkey	25	52	+109
Dairy products	466	295	−37
Fats/oils	46	53	+15
Fruits			
Fresh	109	78	−29
Total processed	44	48	+11
Canned	22	20	−6
Frozen	4.3	10.6	+142
Dried	4.1	1.8	−56
Frozen juice	13.5	15.6	+16
Vegetables			
Fresh	115	98	−15
Total processed	44	61	+38
Canned	41	52	+25
Frozen	3.2	9.6	+200
Potatoes	119	125	+5
Cereal/grain	181	149	−17
Sugar	100.6	102.4	+1.8

Source: E. Binkerd, Armour & Co., Chicago, Ill.

scare. This is unfortunate, since it has also reduced our dietary intake of calcium in proportion to phosphorus. As noted, we eat less fresh fruits and vegetables. The deficiency has been counteracted by an increased consumption of processed vegetables but not of fruits. The vitamin C and vitamin A deficiency problem shown in Table 21.1 is the result of this reduced consumption. Less cereals are consumed but more fats and oils, presumably unsaturated, are being eaten. The lowered consumption of cereals is indicated by the iron problem in Table 21.1.

Much more dental caries was found in the Ten State Nutrition Survey, however, the consumption of sugar has not changed drastically. Possibly the high cost of dental care is the problem.

Over-nutrition

As indicated in Chapter 4, close to 30% of the population is overweight to some degree. The reasons for this will be discussed in the next chapter. The problem is compounded by lack of good education on nutrition and loss of control over diet. Americans eat almost one out of every 3 meals away from home, most of these being served without a vegetable or salad. We also increased our consumption of soft drinks from 158 cans per person in 1950 to 388 cans per person in 1971. Snack foods amounted to 50 lb/person/yr, close to 3% of the diet. This seems small, but it is the overweight population that is probably eating more than their share.

We have also become obsessed with vitamin pills. Many feel if they don't eat right, as long as they take their vitamins, they are all right. This leads to an imbalance in food intake and really wastes money since a good diet can supply the nutrients needed. It should be obvious from the early chapters that vitamins alone do not supply good nutrition.

Menus were expanded to include Sandwich, Soup, Milk, and Fruit.

CHAPTER 22

Obesity and Weight Control

Obesity

"During the past 25 years interest in weight reduction in the United States has grown from a moderate concern to an overriding preoccupation. At present, interest in obesity almost assumes the dimensions of a national neurosis. It would be a pleasure to report that this concern has resulted in new and more effective measures of obesity control or even in more effective use of old measures, but we have no evidence of any decrease in the incidence or severity of obesity. The major result of our national preoccupation has been to worry large numbers of mildly obese persons whose conditions present no real health hazard. It has done nothing about the prevalence of severe obesity among the poor." The preceding statement was made by Albert J. Stunkard in his article, "The Obese: Background and Programs," one of the articles in the book *United States Nutrition Policies* edited by Jean Mayer. (W. H. Freeman & Co., San Francisco. 1973.)

Obesity is not a new problem but has been with us for centuries. Many painters of the 15th, 16th, and 17th centuries used obese people as their subjects and these models for the painters were usually rich members of the ruling class. Plump ladies with large breasts were desirable. At the present the *thin look* seems to have completely reversed the image as to what look is desirable.

Problems and Causes of Obesity.—Obviously, obesity results from the diet. *Calories in = calories out = no weight change* is the principal formula for weight control. If the amount of calories consumed within a diet is equal to the amount of calories expended in the various forms of energy, no weight change will result. However, if "calories in" is greater then "calories out," weight increase will result. Conversely, if "calories in" is less than "calories out" weight decrease results. Tables for these two factors are found in Chapter 2.

The subject of weight control, therefore, concerns weight increase or weight decrease. From a health point of view, a weight decrease can be of more severe medical consequence than a weight increase. The problem in the United States is essentially a weight increase and reflects the fact that Americans consume more calories than are expended.

Calorie (energy) sources exist in foods in the form of fats, proteins, carbohydrates and alcohol. No energy is available from water, cellulose, minerals or vitamins. However, minerals and vitamins are key factors in the breakdown and utilization of energy in the entire biological process of controlling energy.

Diagnosis of Obesity.—One of the most obvious criteria for diagnosing obesity is appearance. However, appearance can be misleading since bulk does not always equate with fat. Muscle mass may give a person a bulky appearance. The second and most widely used criterion for determining obesity is the measurement of skin-fold thickness. By picking up a portion of flesh behind the upper arm and measuring the thickness of this fat layer, a doctor can determine how much fat is on the body. This method of testing is not entirely valid because of the variables in the amounts of flesh measured in the area chosen to be measured and because fat is not always evenly distributed over the body.

Body fat can also be x-rayed, but this is not a desirable procedure for a nationwide survey due to the inability to x-ray enough people and the adverse effects of x-radiation. Comparing body weights with established standards is also utilized. Weight standards for people of given ages and heights indicating desirable weights are derived by many life insurance companies. Whether these standards are representative of all facets of society is questionable.

Definition of Obesity.—Up to 15% bulk above the standard weight is considered to overweight and between 15 to 20% bulk above the standard weight is considered to be obese.

Disadvantages of Obesity.—One of the primary disadvantages to obesity is the inherent health hazard. The mortality rate among the obese increases significantly in proportion to the percent the person is over his standard weight. Table 22.1 shows this increase in mortality with increased obesity. An association between obesity and heart disease exists to the extent that

TABLE 22.1
EFFECT OF OVERWEIGHT ON DEATH RATE

% Overweight	% Increase in Death Rate
10	10–15
20	20–25
30	40–45
40	70

obesity is considered to be responsible in part for the very
high incidence of heart disease in the United States. There is
also a correlation between obesity and diabetes, obese people
being more prone to diabetes. Surgical problems exist with
the obese and often surgeons will insist that weight loss be
substantial before surgery is approved.

The social disadvantages of obesity are indicated by an element of social rejection among obese people. This is especially evident during adolescence when obesity can create
psychological problems for the child.

Why Does a Person Become Obese?— There are many non-
nutritional reasons for people becoming obese, but in the final
analysis, food, in terms of more calories in than calories out,
is the major cause. There are several reasons for the incidence of obesity and overeating: (1) environmental factors,
(2) psychological factors, and (3) physiological factors.

One of the environmental factors includes the availability
of food. If food is readily available, calories are also readily
available, and the likelihood that "calories in" will be more
than "calories out" is very great. The high standard of living
in this country and Western Europe can be attributed to the
availability of food, which leads to high incidence of obesity.
Obesity is not a major factor in African, Asian, and South
American countries. In many of these countries the reverse
is true: caloric intake is less than caloric output, and therefore a weight loss results. At this point *malnutrition* should
be defined accurately. Technically, the entire world is malnourished for the most part. The developing countries are
essentially malnourished due to a lack of calories and high-
quality protein. However, the same definition can be applied
to people in the United States and Western Europe because of

the intake of too many calories. Most of the nutritional diseases and effects of diet on Americans and Western Europeans are caused by too much food rather than too little, which is a form of over-nutrition or malnutrition.

Another environmental factor of obesity reflects the comfort of the environment. In the United States we live in air-conditioned houses, take elevators, and drive cars, limiting the amount of physical activity to almost zero. Figures relating to activities of tribes in East Africa are as follows. Individuals from the ages of 10 to 19 years walk or run over 15 miles in a 12-hr period. Up until the age of 29 these men are the warriors of the tribe. At age 30 they become farmers, but still walk an average of over 10 miles a day. At age 50 and older they are still walking or running approximately 5 miles a day. These people were studied because fat and all the factors that are nutritionally related to heart disease in Americans are consumed in large quantities by East Africans. They eat all kinds of foods, food with higher levels of saturated fats, and they eat more calories. However, the basic equation of caloric intake minus caloric output shows they are not consuming more calories than are being used. This points out the need for physical exercise if the diet is not restricted. These people are not obese and do not suffer from heart disease. Our environment is comfortable, we do not exercise enough, we become obese and suffer the consequences.

Another factor is the psychology of using food to show hospitality. The extent of one's hospitality or friendship is frequently determined by the quality of the food. If a young man is trying to gain the interest and attention of a young female he will often suggest food. Essentially, food serves as a good introduction. If one wants to make friends feel welcome in his home, he serves them food. We have become accustomed to socializing over dinner.

Family and cultural food habits are both environmental and psychological factors. The type of food habits generated in the home are frequently carried on from one generation to the next. What were considered to be suitable nutritional habits in one generation may prove to be extremely unsuitable in the following generation as a result of changes in levels of activity.

Decreased activity includes the reduction of physical activities like walking and running, climbing stairs, etc., due to the increased conveniences of modern life.

Response to external stimuli is another psychological and environmental factor. This means that many people do not eat when they are hungry but instead respond to external stimuli like the clock. On the other hand, many people when unhappy will relieve their tensions by excessive eating.

The last of the psychological and environmental factors is the pattern established in infant feeding. Some researchers believe that patterns in infant feeding can lay down the cause for future obesity. Some studies with rats report that an over-abundance of fat in the diet causes more fat cells to be formed during infancy. This excess of cells will lead to overweight in later life. This work cannot be done experimentally on humans and thus observations must be taken from different animal studies. Studies with piglets show the opposite effect. What proves true for one animal species may not be true for another, and the consumer must take care as to which results and facts to believe. The nutritionist must learn to sift out the real answers.

Quite possibly the "clean plate" syndrome and "just dessert" club that mothers insist on for their children may be a primary causative factor. What is meant by this is that many parents insist on children finishing all their food on the plate *or else*, or finishing it before being treated to a dessert. If the dessert were a piece of fruit this would not be so bad. These factors are hard to pinpoint scientifically.

The physiological factors of obesity are three-fold: (1) decreased basal energy needs, (2) unbalanced secretion of endocrine glands, and (3) genetic propensities toward obesity. The basal metabolic energy requirements decrease as one grows older and, therefore, caloric requirements decrease. In many individuals the older one grows the more food is consumed, and the problem ensues. In some cases of obesity (less than 2%) the hormone secretion of certain endocrine glands becomes unbalanced and this can affect weight control. Why this occurs is not very clear. It may also cause a disorder of the appetite control mechanism so one is constantly hungry.

Lastly, about 3% of obesity can be traced to unknown hereditary factors. There is plenty of evidence that children of fat parents are also fat, but this could be environmental and psychological. Overall, it can be shown that 95% of overweight problems are due to overeating, resulting in "calories in" being greater than "calories out."

Weight Control

Weight-reducing Diets.—Several factors are important in a desirable weight-reducing diet:

(1) It must be deficient in calories. A reduction of 1 lb of body fat tissue means a reduction in 3500 intake calories.

(2) It must be adequate in all nutrients except calories.

(3) It must have a satisfying feeling.

(4) It must be easily adaptable.

(5) It must be a reasonable cost.

(6) It must be a diet that can be eaten over a long period of time.

(7) It should not stress rapid weight loss (allow no more than about 2 to 3 lb to be lost per week).

(8) It should include some form of physical exercise.

(9) It must be different from the previous diet.

(10) It must form the basis of new eating habits.

The basic equation "calories in = calories out" resulting in a reduction in caloric intake is necessary to effect a weight loss. As energy is present in fats, proteins, carbohydrates, and alcohol, a reduction in each of these areas should lead to a reduction in obesity.

Weight-loss Aids.—Dietary aids are currently on the market to assist in the weight reduction for obese people. Chemical agents that reduce food intake are compounds which depress the appetite. These can be desirable, but *only* under medical supervision; otherwise, their use can lead to dangerous consequences. Stimulants such as amphetamines, which are used to suppress appetite, are highly undesirable unless prescribed by a physician. Loss of body water as the result of the use of diuretics is not effective in losing body tissue, because body weight is reduced only by loss of body water. When the body water is replaced by drinking, the body weight goes back to the original amount. Bulk-producing substances are those products which when added to the diet produce a *full* sensation. They do not change dietary habits, however, and most people on these regimens eventually go back to being overweight.

Sauna belts and various instruments for massaging fat away are under investigation by various regulatory agencies. They do nothing to remove fat tissue. Exercise of muscles will help, since it burns up fat tissue for energy. Caloric intake usually does not increase with a mild increase in exercise. Devices that move you have little effect. One hour of vigorous exercise a day can remove 3 lb each month.

Diet Organizations.—Several organizations have been formed to help people lose weight. They all stress social contact, reduction in calories, and exercise to varying degrees. One of them, *TOPS* (Take Off Pounds Sensibly), has had about a 10% success. Another, *Counterweight*, stresses teaching changes in psychological habits toward food and a change in eating habits. A reducing diet is consumed on alternate days amounting to about 1000 calories. This diet is adjusted so that the only reduction is in calories, not in vitamins or minerals. On the other days, a diet equivalent to the caloric needs of the final desired body weight is consumed. This helps to teach the person new eating habits. Exercise is also stressed. The success of this program is not known as yet.

Fad Diets.— The fad diets are the worst violators of the above principles of good diet. They are usually formulated by unknowledgeable people who want to make a profit. The diets promise quick weight loss, with little reduction in food intake, and taking the inches off where desired. Nothing could be further from the truth. Most people gain right back to their original weight when they go off the fad diet. In addition, these diets are dangerous since they usually stress eating an unbalanced diet, such as low carbohydrate, low fat, grapefruit and eggs, etc. Some clinical nutritionists feel that these imbalances eventually lead to physiological changes that can cause heart disease, kidney disease, diabetes, and possible hormonal imbalance.

An example of how ridiculous these diets are is in the claim of being able to lose 10 to 25 lb in one week. To lose even 10 lb of body fat tissue would mean a reduction in caloric intake of 35,000 cal. A person eating even 3500 calories per day would only consume 25,000 calories in a week. Therefore that person would not only have to starve completely, but would have to walk continuously 24 hr a day to burn the additional calories over and above the basal metabolic rate. Obviously, the weight loss reported was mostly due to water losses.

Cutting down on food intake a little at a time can also help to reduce weight and change the diet if the food is not replaced. For example, drinking two less cups of coffee with sugar per day (substitute with water or drink black) will result in about a 14-lb weight loss in one year. If one-half of a slice of toast or bread is cut out, a reduction of 4 lb per year will result. If the diet were analyzed in this way one could easily establish a good weight-reduction program that would work and still supply good nutrition.

CHAPTER 23

Organic and Natural Food

Natural and Organic Foods

Most foods are organic from a chemical standpoint since, as seen in earlier chapters, foods are basically composed of carbon, hydrogen, oxygen, and nitrogen, unless we consider the minerals such as salt which is a minor dietary contribution. In the vernacular, *organic or natural foods* refer to foods that are minimally processed or have not been processed at all. In many cases, due to the lack of processing, organic foods may have a shelf-life much shorter than similar foods that are processed. The quality of organic foods may be worse, as good as, or better than other foods. Organic fruits and vegetables are those foods which are grown on soil that has not been chemically fertilized. They also must not have been sprayed with pesticides. Many FDA investigations reveal that there are as much or more levels of pesticides in organic foods as in regular foods as a result of much dishonesty among the merchants of organic foods who sell regular produce as organic. Certain organizations try to maintain the integrity of true organic foods.

Growth of the Organic Food Market. —The organic and natural food business has been more than doubling every year. Why has this occurred? There are a number of different reasons: a loss of faith in society among young and old due to disappointments in business and government; a negative view of corporation advertising has been evident because of many exaggerations; the enormous increase in the price of food during the '70's—all have turned people off of the regular food supply. Whatever the cause, the result has been an expanding interest in natural home-grown foods and in some cases, the encouragement of organization of food cooperatives to purchase foods in quantity to eliminate the cost of the middleman. The ecology and pollution movement has also increased the resistance to processed foods. The feeling is that the air and water have been polluted, thus leading to the supposition that the food

161

supply is also polluted with unnatural and poisonous additives.
James Turner, the author of *The Chemical Feast*, stated much
this same thing in his book. The people following this theory
feel that the FDA is not doing its job and that millions of Americans are being poisoned. It is interesting to note that, as a
result of more stringent controls and practices, the average
amount of pesticides found in foods decreased in 1973 to less
than 60% of that found in 1967, contrary to popular opinion.
The need for and safety of additives was pointed out in Chapters
17 and 20.

The oldest cause for the organic food movement is the search
for *magic cures*. Many gullible people are fed by quacks and
unknowledgeable food faddists who take existing nutrition facts
and expand them to suit their own selfish needs. In the 1500's
and 1600's country doctors had magic cures which greatly re-
semble many of the diets and dietary prescriptions advocated
by current food *experts*. For example, vitamins from natural
sources are touted as being superior, yet there is no difference
between synthetic and natural vitamins since they are the same
chemical. However, prices can vary by as much as $1000 for
the same amount of vitamin, as is the case with vitamin C. A
year's supply of vitamin C in 100 mg tablets extracted from
rose hips costs as much as $1250 at a health food store on
Park Avenue in New York City. The same amount of synthetic
vitamin C from a local discount department store would cost
under $7.00. They are the same, yet the health food store
makes a large profit. Many unreasonable practices such as
using foods to cure cancer have also been perpetrated on gullible people.

The religious aspect behind health foods is important and not
entirely unfounded. From birth, no matter what religion, the
importance of food is ingrained in people. Many vegetarians
quote the Bible (Genesis, Chapter 1, verse 29) as giving the
basis for vegetarianism and no food additives, but the Bible
(Genesis, Chapter 9, verse 3 to 4) also states that man can eat
meat. Vegetarians can consume an adequate diet with careful
study of the foods which contain the essential nutrients, especially protein, and balancing them carefully.

Whatever the cause, the outcome of the entire organic food
movement has been a new emphasis on rechecking the safety
of additives and more attention to nutrition education. This is

a positive benefit. It is also interesting that many soy non-meat products were developed for vegetarians and various religious sects. These products have been in more demand recently due to shortages of meat supplies. In the future, more and more vegetable substitutes for meat will be used by everyone.

Health Food Stores

Generally, most health food stores, especially in shopping centers, are similar to supermarkets in that foods are well-labeled and very commercial in appearance. The stores usually cater to those who are looking for special foods to cure some ailment. The main problem is that some of the store owners give medical advice which is not factual. The most common *cure* prescribed by store personnel is some type of vitamin taken in large doses. As was seen earlier, this is either wasteful or dangerous. Prices for these vitamins (from natural sources) are usually also 2 to 3 times higher than a comparable vitamin at a department store. Protein tablets are sold in some places which are nothing but compressed dry milk costing 50 times as much as a box of non-fat dry milk from a supermarket.

Cooperatives.—Many cooperatives have been formed to buy foods in large quantities to take advantage of wholesale prices. Two kinds of cooperatives are in operation. A suburban cooperative is generally formed by groups of residents who have become disenchanted with supermarkets and who have arranged to buy processed foods in large quantities. These surburban cooperatives generally serve as distribution centers for these foods.

Other co-ops are formed by volunteers who work together to try to make foods available at lower costs. Due to a lack of knowledge about sanitation many of these stores have had difficulties. These stores claim to sell foods that are natural and organic. In some cases this is true. However, some of the stores sell poor quality food as organic, since it is usually damaged. Bruised or damaged produce looks *organic* because it does not look as perfect and as *plastic* as processed produce.

"Ma and Pa" Organic Food Stores.—This kind of store is primarily aimed at supplying a high quality of food that does

not contain food additives for those who do not want that risk.
The variety of these foods is usually limited to several kinds
of beans, nuts, cereals, unrefined oil, eggs (usually fertile eggs,
though they have not been proved to be any better nutritionally),
wheat germ, certified raw milk, plus organic fruits and vegetables. Prices are usually high due to the higher costs of the
special handling needed for these foods to maintain their quality.
Much of the fresh produce is certified by the OGBA.

Organic Food Production

The OGBA (Organic Growers and Buyers Association) has
approximately 2000 farms in the association. The association
requires a history of the soil utilized for the production of
organic fruits and vegetables to ascertain that it is pesticide-
free and has not been subjected to chemical fertilizers. Animal
manure or green manure is used for fertilization. The foods
are also usually tested to make sure there was no chance contamination with pesticides. It is interesting to note that the use
of chemical fertilization or fertilization with manure makes no
difference to the plant itself. The growth and metabolic processes of a plant take nutrients from the soil only in the form
of mineral salts, not in the form of organic material. The plant
obtains all its oxygen and carbon from the water in the soil
and the carbon dioxide in the air. Nitrogen is taken up in the
form of nitrate salts which are the basic ingredients of chemical fertilizers. Bacteria in the soil act to change organic
fertilizers (green manure) into inorganic matter to be used
subsequently by the plant. Therefore, from the standpoint of
minerals utilized by the plant, there are no advantages to
organic farming except that it is a good way to recycle organic
waste matter.

Some differences between the effects of chemical and organic
fertilizers do exist. Yields are higher with chemical fertilizers
due to a more complete saturation of the soil. Nitrate run-off,
which is a major cause of water pollution, is also greater with
chemical fertilizers. Problems in using animal manure occur
also. Cases of contamination of fruits and vegetables with
Salmonella have occurred. The possibility also exists that, in
organic culture, plants take up large quantities of heavy metals

such as mercury which can be detrimental to the consumer. This is because the soils may not be in the proper condition to oxidize the metals into a state in which they would not be absorbed by the plant. Proper composting of green manure would prevent this.

Vegetarian Diets

A vegetarian who has sound nutritional education can benefit from a vegetarian diet. Surveys show that the incidence of heart disease among well-educated vegetarians is approximately 10 times less than for people who utilize meat in their diet. Weights of these people usually indicate that they are 20 lb under the standard for people of their average height and their cholesterol levels are usually 30% lower than that of normal meat eaters.

Uneducated vegetarians are sometimes vegetarians because meat is unavailable; as a result of inadequately balanced protein in the diet, they will become malnourished. Vegetarians can be classified into three types: (1) vegans, those who eat fruits, nuts and vegetables exclusively; (2) ovo-vegetarians, those who consume the vegan diet plus eggs; and (3) lacto-vegetarians, those who supplement the vegan diet with milk and milk products and sometimes eggs. The ovo and lacto vegetarians can be very successful vegetarians because essential amino acids are consumed from the dairy products and eggs. The vegans have the greatest difficulty in eating a balanced diet because of the poor quality and low amounts of protein found in vegetables.

Vegetarians are often said to have anemia caused by a vitamin B_{12} deficiency since they don't eat meat, the main source of this vitamin. If one started out as a vegetarian at birth this would be a problem. Most vegetarians who consume milk and eggs are able to obtain their B_{12} requirement. If one ate only vegetables an anemic condition due to vitamin B_{12} deficiency would probably not become evident until 3 to 5 years after the commencement of the diet. The body is capable of storing the B_{12} vitamin for a period of time and using it only slowly. Doctors and nutritionists generally suggest that vegetarians obtain a vitamin B_{12} injection once a year or eat brewers' yeast as a source of B_{12}.

Another source of protein for vegetarians is soy. Problems exist, however, in that some soy products contain natural carbohydrates which the body cannot digest. These sugars are acted upon by the bacteria in the large intestine, releasing great amounts of gas. This is especially common in male vegetarians. Methods for removing these sugars are being tested by the food industry.

Zen Macrobiotic Diet

Zen macrobiotics is a term that is much maligned by people both for and against Zen macrobiotics. It has caught on in the counterculture and has become quite popular. The diet was started by George Ohsawa who tried to initiate the diet in the United States but failed to do so. The goal of the Zen macrobiotic diet, as set down by Ohsawa, is the achievement of a calm soul through dietary practices. He professed that the diet, in conjunction with the inner calmness of the soul, can overcome any illness. His diet is based on the opposing forces of the Oriental philosophy of Taoism. The opposing forces are the Yin and the Yang. The diet has no connection to Zen Buddhism. Ohsawa felt that one had to have a certain ratio of yin to yang, and reclassified various foods on this basis.

The Zen macrobiotic diet consists of 10 levels (−3 to 7). The beginning level, level −3, is a very well-balanced diet consisting of meats, vegetables, cereals, etc. Level 7 should only be used in specific circumstances and consists solely of cereal grains with very little water intake. The latter point is where brown rice has been given so much attention. Ohsawa ranked brown rice as having the best Yin-Yang ratio and therefore suggested that on level 7 only brown rice should be eaten. Brown rice lacks vitamin C, is low in protein and the protein quality is poor (Table 6.2). There is no difference in protein content between brown and white rice. In order to acquire the recommended daily allowance of protein by eating rice, it would be necessary to eat at least 2 lb a day.

The Zen macrobiotic diet and philosophy is supposed to cure all diseases. If it fails to do so, Ohsawa stated that is because there is not enough faith among the practitioners or because the person has not practiced the diet long enough. There have been several cases of death resulting from the Zen macrobiotic

diet because of lack of vitamin C and consequent loss of resistance to disease. It is not the purpose of this book to criticize
the religion *per se* but only to educate against the health haz-
ards involved in a diet that does not supply the body with adequate nutrients.

I   RAW MATERIALS ACQUISITION

*Maintenance of raw material
flow at optimum level.
Quality control. Proper storage
prior to conveyance to
the production line.*

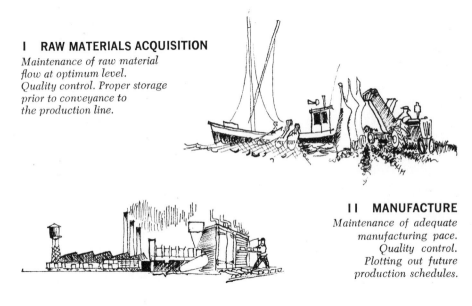

II   MANUFACTURE

*Maintenance of adequate
manufacturing pace.
Quality control.
Plotting out future
production schedules.*

I I I   DISTRIBUTION

*Maintenance of steady,
timely distribution to consumer
centers. Quality control
through proper storage,
shipping, market conditions.*

Divisions and Functions in the Food Industry

Recommended Books

This book has tried to cover the nature of the relationship of food to man, hopefully "Food For Thought," which is both entertaining and educational. We have learned about the chem- icals that compose food and how they are broken down and metabolized in the body. The nutritional requirements of the body were also pointed out. The book has covered the why's and how's of processed food, information that many have no knowledge of. This should supply a better understanding of the value and safety of our food supply. The nutritional prob- lems in the United States have been covered in terms of fad diets, obesity and diseases. An overall picture of food has been given to furnish a basis for making wise and reasonable choices as to our diet and also help counter the many fallacious claims made by faddist, dieters and others in general conver- sations. For those who wish to do more reading this chapter lists some recommended texts:

*ARLIN, M. T. 1972. The Science of Nutrition. Macmillan Co., New York.

BENARDE, M. A. 1970. The Chemicals We Eat. American Heritage Press, New York.

CARTER, R. 1964. Your Food and Your Health. Harper and Row, New York.

CHANEY, M. S. and ROSS, M. L. 1966. Nutrition, 7th Edition, Houghton & Co., Boston.

*CLYDESDALE, F., and FRANCIS, J. 1976. Food Nutrition and You. Prentice Hall, New York.

CRAMPTON, E., and LLOYD, L. 1959. Fundamentals of Nutrition. W. H. Freeman & Co., San Francisco.

*DAVIDSON, S., PASSMORE, R., and BROCK, J. F. 1972. Human Nutrition and Dietetics, 5th Edition. Williams & Wilkins Co., Baltimore.

*DEUTSCH, R. 1962. The Nuts Among the Berries. Ballantine Books, New York.

*DEUTSCH, R. 1971. The Family Guide to Better Food and Better Health. Bantam Books, New York.

DEUTSCH, R. 1976. The Realities of Nutrition. Bull Publishing Co., Palo Alto.

*Books Highly Recommended

*GERARD, R. W. 1965. Food for Life. University of Chicago Press, Chicago.

HARRIS, R. S., and KARMAS, E. 1975. Nutritional Evaluation of Food Processing, 2nd Edition. AVI Publishing Co., Westport, Conn.

HUTCHINSON, R. C. 1958. Food for Better Living. Cambridge University, New York.

JACOBSON, M. 1973. Eaters' Digest. Ballantine Books, New York.

**LABUZA, T. P. 1975. The Nutrition Crisis. West Publishing Co., St. Paul.

*LABUZA, T. P. 1977. Food and Your Well Being. West Publishing Co., and the AVI PUBLISHING CO., Westport, Conn.

LAMB, M. W., and HARDEN, M. 1973. The Meaning of Human Nutrition. Pergamon Press, Inc., New York.

*LEVERTON, R. M. 1965. Food Becomes You, 3rd Edition. Iowa State University Press, Ames, Iowa.

MCHENRY, E. E. 1960. Foods Without Fads. J. B. Lippincott Co., Philadelphia.

MFG. CHEMISTS ASSOC. Food Additives–What They are, How They are Used. Washington, D. C.

NASSET, E. S. 1962. Your Diet, Digestion and Health, 2nd Edition. Barnes and Noble, New York.

*POTTER, N. N. 1973. Food Science, 2nd Edition. AVI Publishing Co., Westport, Conn.

ROBINSON, C. H. 1965. Basic Nutrition and Diet Therapy. Macmillan Co., New York.

*RUNYON, THORA. 1976. Nutrition for Today. Harper and Row, New York.

SALMON, M. B. 1965. Food Facts for Teenagers. C. C. Thomas Co., Springfield, Illinois.

SEBRELL, W. H., JR., HAGGERTY, J. J., and THE EDITORS OF LIFE. 1967. Food and Nutrition. TIME–LIFE BOOKS, Chicago.

*SMITH, N. 1976. Food for Sport. Bull Publishing Co., Palo Alto.

*STEWART, G., and AMERINE, M. A. 1973. Introduction to Food Science. Academic Press, New York.

SPOCK, D., and LOWENBERG, M. 1956. Feeding Your Baby and Child. Pocket Books, New York.

TATKON, M. D. 1968. The Great Vitamin Hoax. Macmillan Co., New York.

TURNER, J. 1970 The Chemical Feast. Grossman Publishing Co., New York.

U.S. DEPT. AGR. Agriculture Handbook #456–Nutritional Value of American Foods in Common Units. U.S. Govt. Printing Office, Washington, D.C.

WAYLER, T. J., and KLEIN, R. S. 1965. Applied Nutrition. Macmillan Co., New York.

*WHITE, P. L. 1974. Let's Talk About Food. The American Medical Assoc., Chicago.

*WILSON, E. D., FISHER, K. H., and FUQUA, M. E. 1974. Principles of Nutrition, 3rd Edition. John Wiley & Sons, New York.

*YOUNG, J. H. 1967. The Medical Messiahs. Princeton University Press.

*Books Highly Recommended

Glossary

Ammonia compressors—Machines which utilize compression of the gas ammonia to produce refrigeration.

Amphetamine—A chemical compound commonly known as "speed"which suppresses the appetite.

Anemia—A condition in which the number of red blood cells in the blood is too low.

Antioxidant—A chemical which retards oxidation and thus inhibits rancidity in a food.

Antitoxin—A chemical compound that inhibits the action of chemicals that are toxic to the human body.

Basal metabolic rate—The amount of energy needed in terms of calories per day that is used to regulate and maintain the body's functions when no voluntary action is taking place.

Blanch—Heating a fruit or vegetable in steam to help destroy enzymes so that the product is stable.

Bond—A chemical term referring to the joining together of two or more elements to form a compound.

Browning, enzymatic—The process whereby a food turns brown or darkens during storage; also applies to non-enzymatic browning, a similar process which is not catalyzed by an enzyme.

Carcinogen—A substance which causes cancer in the body.

Catalysis—The process whereby the chemical reaction is greatly accelerated by the presence of a certain chemical (catalyst) which is not consumed in the reaction.

Comminuted product—A product which is ground up or mashed into small pieces. Hamburger is a type of comminuted product.

Dental caries—The occurrence of cavities in teeth due in part to diet.

Dialysis—In reference to kidney disease a technique whereby the blood stream is cleansed of undesirable compounds by passing the blood through a permeable membrane.

Emulsion—In reference to foods, usually a mixture of fat droplets suspended in water. Milk is an emulsion.

Endocrine glands—Specific glands in the human body that excrete hormones.

Enzyme—A protein compound that helps enable chemical reactions in the body to go on at a faster rate; an organic catalyst.

Filtration—A process whereby a solution is cleaned of suspended material by passing it through a fine screen or permeable membrane.

Foam—A mixture of air in a solution usually containing protein
and fat that produces a fluffy structure.

Folic acid—A class of water-soluble vitamin contained mostly
in green vegetables.

Free radicals—Chemical entities produced during a reaction
causing rancidity of foods. They are very reactive, that is,
they are unstable and will easily initiate chain reactions such
as oxidation.

Freezer burn—The loss of water from the surface of a frozen
food resulting in a darkening of the area and undesirable
appearance and texture.

Gas chromatograph—An instrument used to isolate and identify
chemical compounds of a food particularly the flavor characteristics.

Green manure—The inedible portions of green plants used to
fertilize the soil.

Gums—Natural compounds which when added to water give
thick, gravy-like textures.

Hormone—A chemical compound produced in the body that helps
to regulate various metabolic functions.

Humectant—A chemical compound like sugar, salt or glycerol
which when added to food helps bind water.

Kilogram—1000 gm or approximately 2.2 lb.

Lymph system—The circulatory system in the body that carries
the lymph secretions throughout the body.

Metabolism—The process whereby foods are converted into
chemical compounds and energy within the body.

Misbranding—The illegal representation of a food under the
Food and Drug Act.

Moisture content—The amount of water present in a food.

Mouth feel—The sensory perception in the mouth of the textural characteristics of a food.

Mutagen—A chemical compound which can cause undesirable
mutations in a living organism.

Osteoporosis—The disease of old age in which calcium has been removed from bones and the bones have become soft and brittle.

Oxalic acid—A toxic chemical found naturally in spinach which can irreversibly react with iron and cause it not to be absorbed during digestion.

Oxidation—The reaction of food compounds with oxygen leading to the production of undesirable flavors, odors and toxic material.

Parts per million (ppm)—A concentration of chemicals in a food which is at a very low level, namely at a level where, for example, 1 ppm means that there is 1 lb of a chemical found in 1 million lb of a food.

Pasteurization—The mild heating of a fluid to reduce the microbial population, and thereby making it safe to consume.

Pathway—A biochemical scheme or series of reactions in which the chemical compound is broken down to produce other compounds in the body.

Peristalsis—The natural involuntary movement of the digestive tract.

Permeable—A membrane which allows certain chemical compounds to pass through it yet retains others.

Peroxides—Chemicals which are produced during the chemical reaction causing rancidity of foods. These compounds break down and cause destruction of nutrients and production of off-flavors and off-odors.

Pigment—The color material that is contained in a food.

Polymers—A large molecule made up of small similar subunits (monomers) joined together.

Prorate—To divide, assess or distribute proportionally.

Pulling a vacuum—The mechanical action of a device which removes the gases from an enclosed vessel.

Retort—A high-pressure steam vessel in which canned foods are commercially sterilized.

Senescence—Natural life process that continues in fruits and vegetables after harvesting that leads to the aging and final decay of the food product.

Shelf-life—The average life time that a food material has once it is stored in the home of the consumer whereby it still has quality and good nutritional value.

Silicates—Chemicals added to food materials such as salt to prevent caking, e.g., calcium silicate.

Slurry—A mixture of solid and liquid materials that form a pasty substance with a texture much like wet cement.

Symbiosis—The living together of two organisms that help produce environmental factors such that each permits the other to live.

Teratogen—A chemical compound that can cause undesirable birth defects much as thalidomide did.

Toxin—A chemical which when ingested can cause bodily harm or disease.

Viscosity—The property of a solution that is characterized by its flowability; a high viscosity food would be mayonnaise, while water is a low viscosity.

Index

Other AVI Books

FOOD SCIENCE AND TECHNOLOGY

BASIC FOOD CHEMISTRY
Lee

CARBOHYDRATES AND HEALTH
Hood, Wardrip and Bollenback

DIETARY NUTRIENT GUIDE
Pennington

DRUG-INDUCED NUTRITIONAL DEFICIENCIES
Roe

ELEMENTARY FOOD SCIENCE
Nickerson and Ronsivalli

ELEMENTS OF FOOD TECHNOLOGY
Desrosier

EVALUATION OF PROTEINS FOR HUMANS
Bodwell

FOOD AND THE CONSUMER
Kramer

FOOD COLLOIDS
Graham

FOOD MICROBIOLOGY: PUBLIC HEALTH
AND SPOILAGE ASPECTS
deFigueiredo and Splittstoesser

FOOD SCIENCE
2nd Edition   *Potter*

FOOD SERVICE SCIENCE
Smith and Minor

FUNDAMENTALS OF FOOD FREEZING
Desrosier and Tressler

IMMUNOLOGICAL ASPECTS OF FOODS
Catsimpoolas

INTRODUCTORY FOOD CHEMISTRY
Garard

LABORATORY MANUAL IN FOOD CHEMISTRY
Woods and Aurand

MENU PLANNING
Eckstein

NUTRITIONAL EVALUATION OF FOOD PROCESSING
2nd Edition   *Harris and Karmas*

SCHOOL FOODSERVICE
Van Egmond

THE STORY OF FOOD
Garard

THE TECHNOLOGY OF FOOD PRESERVATION
4th Edition   *Desrosier and Desrosier*